Do's and Taboos
Around The World

Edited by Roger E. Axtell

Compiled by  THE PARKER PEN COMPANY

with offices in 154 countries

A BENJAMIN BOOK

JOHN WILEY & SONS, Inc.

New York • Chichester • Brisbane • Toronto • Singapore

TO GET ADDITIONAL COPIES

For promotion recommendations and discount pricing on special printing or large quantities, contact:

The Benjamin Company, Inc.
One Westchester Plaza   OR   12000 West Park Place
Elmsford, NY 10523   Milwaukee, WI 53224
(914) 592-8088   (414) 466-2120

Produced by The Benjamin Company, Inc.
One Westchester Plaza
Elmsford, New York 10523

Library of Congress Catalog Number: 85-072038

Library of Congress Cataloging-in-Publication Data

Do's and taboos around the world.

   Includes index.
   1. Business etiquette.   2. Intercultural communication.

I. Axtell, Roger E.   II. Parker Pen Company.
HF5387.D66   1986   395'.52   86-15977
ISBN 0-471-85356-9
Illustrations by Robert Weber   Cover Illustration by Robert Weber
              Howard Munce
                                             Designed by: Bass & Goldman
                                             Typography by: Computer Careers, Inc.

Printed in the United States of America

    87   10   9   8   7   6   5   4   3   2

Contents

How do you gracefully sample a dish of gorilla? When does a nod mean no? Where is it a handshake instead of a kiss? Diplomacy isn't just for diplomats — how you behave in other people's countries reflects not only on you, but on the image of the company, and the country, that you represent.

Actions speak louder than words, and often say all the wrong things. Eye contact, hand gestures, touching, bowing — the inappropriate signal can signify disaster. To help guide you through touchy occasions, this chapter includes an illustrated international dictionary of gestures.

For the fast-moving international executive and the casual tourist alike, this quick reference list offers the key do's and don'ts to know when visiting foreign lands. Arranged alphabetically by region and country.

Preface

It was the mid-1960s and the voice of Gamal Abdel Nasser issued from the radio while a fan waved slowly overhead. The house was large, white, and stucco, with marble floors providing some coolness.

Eight men were seated in a circle, some on overstuffed cushions, some on thick frieze chairs reminiscent of a Ginger Rogers movie.

Someone passed the wooden mouthpiece of the hookah, a water pipe with a long hose not unlike a vacuum cleaner hose. The hose was connected to a large bubbling beaker with tobacco burning in a bowl situated on top. The pipe was passed slowly around the room, mouth to mouth.

The group comprised seven brothers and one young and rather naive American businessman. The brothers all wore long Arab robes and were important customers. No women were in sight. No alcohol. And Nasser's emotional Arabic coming from the radio reminded the young American of the delicate politics hanging over the occasion. For someone born in Wisconsin, this was a most unfamiliar setting and extremely important business occasion.

Two thoughts prevailed. First, avoid any social blunders in this most important moment. Second, get back to the hotel room and make notes on proper behavior and this extraordinary evening.

That vignette — the hookah, the robes, the need to make notes — was, perhaps, the origin of this book.

The need and opportunity for Americans to travel abroad are even stronger today than in the 1960s. And so is the need to avoid faux pas. More than ever, the marketplace is global. Americans *must* move abroad, and move effectively, comfortably, and with the highest respect for other cultures.

The problem is that the rules for proper behavior are not very exact.

This book is *not* an anthropological study of *why* different peoples around the world behave in different ways. Instead, its purpose is to create an awareness of, or sensitivity to, behavior when one is traveling outside the United States or dealing in this country with a visitor from overseas. (Notice the word "foreigner" has been avoided? Who likes to be called a "foreigner"? We might label that as lesson number one.)

Ideally, this book will help each world traveler grow little invisible antennae that will sense incoming messages about cultural differences and nuances. An appreciation and under-standing of these differences will prevent embarrassment, unhappiness, and failure. In fact, learning through travel about these cultural differences can be both challenging and fun.

This book is not — repeat, not — the definitive book on proper behavior. Some readers will say, "Oh, but that gesture or that practice may apply in the North of that country, but not in the South." And they may be right. This book is a compilation of surveys, research, and personal experiences in an area of study — human behavior — where there is never precise definition. You'll also find, because of our diverse sources, some variations in writing style.

Corrections, refinements, improvements, or additions are encouraged and welcomed. Send them to:

> S. Gies, Editor
> John Wiley & Sons, Inc.
> 605 Third Avenue
> New York, NY 10158

Then watch for an improved and even more informative second edition.

ROGER E. AXTELL

Acknowledgments

A compendium like this could not possibly be completed without the minds and hands of many people. The following alphabetical list acknowledges the contributions of those foremost among our contributors.

Brigham Young University's Center for International Area Studies is one of the few — and finest — resources available for the type of cultural information offered in this book. Such conscientious research and sensitivity to national behavior is a tribute to the evangelical work of the Mormon Church.

Scott M. Cutlip has had no direct involvement in this book. Instead, as the "grand seigneur" and dean of educators in public relations, he has instilled a profound responsibility within anyone who has practiced that craft since World War II. Coauthor of the first comprehensive textbook on public relations, he has been mentor, friend, and inspiration to the editor of this book.

Richard W. Holznecht was both supporter and contributor. He has a unique capability for nonconventional expression and his credo has been, when weaving words, strive for uniqueness and grace. He possesses that talent in unfair abundance.

Ian Kerr, President, Press Relations Services, Greenwich, Connecticut, is a public relations consultant for major companies on both sides of the Atlantic. Born and educated in England, he has spent his career educating and serving clients in all forms of communications — with words and all other wisdom. He contributed large portions of both those commodities to this book.

Daniel Parker, Honorary Chairman of The Parker Pen Company, not only guided the company until 1966 but then headed the prestigious National Association of Manufacturers (NAM) and later directed the U.S. government's Agency for International Development under Secretary of State Henry Kissinger. In those roles he has traveled the world extensively and imbued everyone around him with a strong sense of internationalism.

George Parker is Chairman of The Parker Pen Company. In 1902 his grandfather foresaw the need for American businessmen to travel and sell their products outside the U.S. During the past 20 years, George has caused the greatest growth cycle in Parker's near 100-year history and was responsible for sending Parker products and Parker travelers into every market of the world where hands hold writing instruments. His success in the tough field of consumer goods, competing against all nations, is an example to all in American business.

Cynthia Proulx and Ian Keown provided the finished writing of the manuscript plus some additional research. Each has spent the last dozen or so years traveling far and wide and writing about it: Ian in frequent magazine features for *Travel & Leisure, Esquire,* and the airline magazines as well as in his own guidebooks *Caribbean Hideaways, Very Special Places,* and *European Hideaways;* Cynthia as a contributor to those guides and in her own magazine and newspaper articles.

Lois Puerner would have made one of the world's best mediators or negotiators because of her boundless patience, dedication, and pleasant disposition. Instead, she is only the finest secretary in the Western Hemisphere and has silently suffered through surveys, rewrites, research, more rewrites, correspondence, and chaos. As the reader skips across the words in this volume in microseconds, pause occasionally in respect to the many times Mrs. Puerner struggled with each one.

Kathleen Kelley Reardon, Ph.D., conducted a survey sponsored by The Parker Pen Company from which the section on gift giving is derived. She is an associate professor of interpersonal and mass media communication in the Department of Communication Sciences at the University of Connecticut.

Eugene G. Rohlman was responsible for much of the text derived from Dr. Reardon's extensive research, plus ideas, support, and enthusiasm over several years. Gene is Public Relations Manager of The Parker Pen Company and the winner of numerous awards for writing, employee publications, and photography. This book would still be in its original womb — an overstuffed cardboard box — without the work and help of Gene Rohlman.

Nina Streitfeld, Vice President, Press Relations Services, has served for two decades in a variety of executive and consultant positions for corporate, government, and nonprofit institutions. With the help of Research Assistant **Sherry Ek,** Nina was responsible for the survey and research in this book's "American Jargon" section.

Robert R. Williams is a bright, witty, and intelligent public relations resource (Idea Associates, Stevens Point, Wisconsin) who provided encouragement and ideas for this volume.

CHAPTER 1

Protocol, Customs,
and
Etiquette

Three Great Gaffes
or
One country's good manners, another's grand faux pas

In Washington, they call protocol "etiquette with a government expense account." But diplomacy isn't just for diplomats. How you behave in other people's countries reflects on more than you alone. It also brightens — or dims — the image of where you come from and whom you work for. The Ugly American about whom we used to read so much may be dead, but here and there the ghost still wobbles out of the closet.

Three well-traveled Americans tell how even an old pro can sometimes make the wrong move in the wrong place at the wrong time.

A partner in one of New York's leading private banking firms

When the board chairman is Lo Win Hao, do you smile brightly and say, "How do you do, Mr. Hao?" Or Mr. Lo? Or Mr. Win?

"I traveled nine thousand miles to meet a client and arrived with my foot in my mouth. Determined to do things right, I'd memorized the names of the key men I was to see in Singapore. No easy job, inasmuch as the names all came in threes. So, of course, I couldn't resist showing off that I'd done my homework. I began by addressing top man Lo Win Hao with plenty of well-placed Mr. Hao's — and sprinkled the rest of my remarks with a Mr. Chee this and a Mr. Woon that. Great show. Until a note was passed to me from one man I'd met before, in New York. Bad news. 'Too friendly too soon, Mr. Long,' it said. Where diffidence is next to godliness, there I was, calling a roomful of VIPs, in effect, Mr. Ed and Mr. Charlie. I'd remembered everybody's name — but forgot that in Chinese the surname comes *first* and the given name *last*."

An associate in charge of family planning for an international human welfare organization

The lady steps out in her dazzling new necklace and everybody dies laughing. (Or what not to wear in Togo on a Saturday night.)

"From growing up in Cuba to joining the Peace Corps to my present work, I've spent most of my life in the Third World. So nobody should know better than I how to dress for it. Certainly one of the silliest mistakes an outsider can make is to dress up in

3

'native' costume, whether it's a sari or a sombrero, unless you really know what you're doing. Yet, in Togo, when I found some of the most beautiful beads I'd ever seen, it never occurred to me not to wear them. While I was upcountry, I seized the first grand occasion to flaunt my new find. What I didn't know is that locally the beads are worn not at the neck but at the waist — to hold up a sort of loincloth under the skirt. So, into the party I strutted, wearing around my neck what to every Togoese eye was part of a pair of underpants."

An account executive at an international data processing and electronics conglomerate

Even in a country run by generals, would you believe a runny nose could get you arrested?

"A friend and I were coming into Colombia on business after a weekend in the Peruvian mountains touring Machu Picchu. What a sight that had been. And what a head cold the change in temperature had given my friend. As we proceeded through Customs at the airport, he was wheezing and blowing into his handkerchief like an active volcano. Next thing I knew, two armed guards were lockstepping him through a door. I tried to intercede before the door slammed shut, but my spotty Spanish failed me completely. Inside a windowless room with the guards, so did his. He shouted in English. They shouted in Spanish. It was beginning to look like a bad day in Bogotá when a Colombian woman who had seen what happened burst into the room and finally achieved some bilingual understanding. It seems all that sniffling in the land of the infamous coca leaf had convinced the guards that my friend was waltzing through their airport snorting cocaine."

Cuddly Ethnocentrics

If only the world's Customs inspectors could train their German shepherds to sniff out the invisible baggage we all manage to slip with us into foreign countries. They are like secret little land mines of the mind. Set to go off at the slightest quiver, they can sabotage a five-minute stroll down the Champs Elysées or a $5,000,000 tractor sale to Peking. Three of our most popular national take-alongs:

Why Don't They Speak English? For the same reason we don't speak Catalan or Urdu. The wonder, in fact, is that so many people do speak so many languages. Seldom is a Continental European fluent in fewer than three, often more. Africans grow up with the language of the nation that once colonized theirs plus half a dozen different tribal dialects. Japan has three distinct Japanese languages, which even the lowliest streetsweeper can understand. Middle Eastern businesspeople shift effortlessly from their native tongue(s) to Oxford English to Quai d'Orsay French. Yet most of the English-speaking world remains as cheerfully monolingual as Queen Victoria's parakeet. If there are any complaints, then, it is clear they should not be coming from the American/English-speaking traveler.

Take Me to Your Burger King. In Peoria, a Parisian does not go looking for pot-au-feu. Alone among travelers, Americans seem to embark like astronauts— sealed inside a cozy life-support system from home. Scrambled eggs. Rent-a-cars. Showers. TV. Nothing wrong with any of it back home, but to the rest of the universe it looks sadly like somebody trying to read a book with the cover closed. Experiment! Try the local specialties.

American Know-How to the Rescue! Our brightest ideas have taken root all over the world — from assembly lines in Düsseldorf to silicon chips in Osaka to hybrid grains that are helping to nourish the Third World. Nonetheless, bigger, smarter, and faster do not inevitably add up to better. Indeed, the desire to take on shiny new American ways has been the downfall of nations whose cultures were already rich in art and technology when North America was still a glacier. As important as the idea itself is the way it is presented.

A U.S. doctor of public health recently back from West Africa offers an example of how to make the idea fit the ideology. "I don't just pop over and start handing out anti-malaria pills on the corner," she says. "First I visit with the village chief. After he gives his blessing, I move in with the local witch doctor. After she shows me her techniques and I show her mine — and a few lives are saved— maybe then we can get the first native to swallow the first pill."

This is as true at the high-tech level as at the village dispensary. "What is all this drinking of green tea before the meeting with Mitsubishi?" The American way is to get right down to business. Yet if you look at Mitsubishi's bottom line, you have to wonder if green tea is such a bad idea after all.

It should come as no surprise that people surrounded by oceans rather than by other people end up ethnocentric. Even our

5

biggest fans admit that America often strikes the rest of the world as a sweet-but-spoiled little darling, wanting desperately to please but not paying too much attention to how it is done. Ever since the Marshall Plan, we seemed to believe that *our* games and *our* rules were the only ones in town. Any town. And that all else was the Heart of Darkness.

Take this scene in a Chinese cemetery. Watching a Chinese reverently placing fresh fruit on a grave, an American visitor asked, "When do you expect your ancestors to get up and eat the fruit?" The Chinese replied, "As soon as your ancestors get up and smell the flowers."

Hands Across the Abyss

Our bad old habits are giving way to a new when-in-Rome awareness. Some corporations take it so seriously that they put employees into a crash course of overseas cultural immersion. AT&T, for instance, encourages — and pays for — the whole family of an executive on his way to a foreign assignment to enroll in classes given by experts in the mores and manners of other lands.

Among the areas that cry out loudest for international understanding are how to say people's names, eat, dress, and talk. Get those four basics right and the rest is a piece of kuchen.

Basic Rule #1: What's in a name?

Goodbye, Notowidigeo. Hello, Sastroamidjojo. At the U.S. State Department, foreign names are almost as crucial as foreign policy. The social secretary to a former secretary of state recalls that even in the relatively unselfconscious 1950s she put herself through a rigorous rehearsal of names before every affair of state. Of all the challenges, she says, the ambassador from what was then Ceylon (now Sri Lanka) was the toughest. After days of practicing "Ambassador Notowidigeo," she was informed that a new man had the job — and was on his way to be received. "You'd be surprised how fast you can memorize Sastroamidjojo when you have to," she adds.

The first transaction between even ordinary citizens — and the first chance to make an impression for better or worse— is, of course, an exchange of names. In America, there usually is not very much to get wrong. And even if you do, so what?

Not so elsewhere. Especially in the Eastern Hemisphere, where name frequently denotes social rank or family status, a mistake can be an outright insult. So can switching to a given name without the other person's permission, even when you think the situation calls for it.

"What would you like me to call you?" is always the opening line of one overseas deputy director for an international telecommunications corporation. "Better to ask several times," he advises, "than to get it wrong." Even then, "I err on the side of formality until asked to 'Call me Joe.'" Another frequent traveler insists his company provide him with a list of key people he will meet, country by country, surnames underlined, to be memorized on the flight over.

Don't trust the rules

Just when you think you have broken the international name code, they switch the rules on you. Take Latin America. Most people's names are a combination of the father's and mother's, with only the father's name used in conversation. In the Spanish-speaking countries, the father's name comes first. Hence, Carlos Mendoza-Miller is called Mr. Mendoza. *But* in Portuguese-speaking Brazil, it is the other way around, with the mother's name first.

In the Orient, the Chinese system of surname first, given name last does not always apply. The Taiwanese, many of whom were educated in missionary schools, often have a Christian first name, which comes before any of the others — as in Tommy Ho Chin, who should be called Mr. Ho or, to his friends, Tommy Ho. Also, given names are often officially changed to initials, and a Y.Y. Lang is Y.Y.; never mind what it stands for. In Korea, which of a man's names takes a Mr. is determined by whether he is his father's first or second son. Although in Thailand names run backwards, Chinese style, the Mr. is put with the *given* name, and to a Thai it is just as important to be called by his given name as it is for a Japanese to be addressed by his surname. With the latter, incidentally, you can in a very friendly relationship respond to his using *your* first name by dropping the Mr. and adding *san* to his last name, as in Ishikawa-san.

Hello. Are you still there? Then get ready for the last installment of the name game, which is to disregard all of the above — sometimes. The reason is that many Easterners who deal regularly with the West are now changing the order of their names to un-confuse us. So, while to each other their names remain the same, to us the given name may come before the surname. Then again, it may not.

The safest course remains: ask.

Don't Leave Home Without It

Overseas, the ultimate passport is the business card — proof that you really do exist. Even a casual exchange of names between tourist and native usually calls for it. Any business contact demands it. Not just because, to a foreigner, your name is foreign and hence easier to absorb in writing, but particularly because rank and profession are taken so much more seriously than here at home. A reporter, for instance, is never called a mere reporter but a *journalist*, with the lofty implications of a James Reston or Eric Sevareid. In Italy, even a bachelor's degree entitles you to put a *Dr.* in front of your name. *Professor* is also used much more loosely than in the U.S. In Asia, it is not so much *who* you are as *where* you are in the pecking order of any given meeting or transaction. Suggestions:

- On the card, include your company name and your position plus any titles such as vice president, manager, associate director. Don't use abbreviations.

- If you are going where English is not widely spoken, take your cards to a printer when you get there and have the reverse side printed in the local language. (In Hong Kong and Tokyo, overnight service is available.)

- In most of Southeast Asia, Africa, and the Middle East (except Israel), never present the card with your left hand.

- In Japan, present it with both hands, and make sure the type is facing the recipient and is right-side-up.

Basic Rule #2: Eat, drink, and be wary.

Pass the gorilla, please. Away from home, eating is more than just a way to keep your pin-striped suit from falling off. It is a language all its own, and no words can match it for saying "Glad to meet you . . . glad to be doing business with you . . . glad to have you here in the beautiful Rann of Kutch" or wherever.

Clearly, mealtime is no time for a thanks-but-no-thanks response. Acceptance of what is on your plate is tantamount to acceptance of host, country, and company. So, no matter how tough things may be to swallow, swallow. Or, as one veteran globe girdler puts it, "Travel with a cast-iron stomach and eat everything everywhere."

Tastiness is in the eye of the beholder

Often, what is offered constitutes your host country's proudest culinary achievements. What would we Americans think of a Frenchman who refused a bite of homemade apple pie or sizzling sirloin? Squeamishness comes not so much from the thing itself as from our unfamiliarity with it. After all, an oyster has remarkably the same look and consistency as a sheep's eye, and at first encounter a lobster would strike almost anybody as more a creature from science fiction than something you dip in melted butter and pop into your mouth.

Incidentally, in Saudi Arabia, sheep's eyes are a delicacy, and in China, it's bear's paw soup.

Perhaps the ultimate in exotic dining abroad befell a family planning expert on a trip for an international human welfare organization. It was a newly emerged African country where the national dish — in fact, the *only* dish eleven months of the year — is yam. The visitor's luck, however, was to be there the *other* month, when gorillas come in from the bush to steal the harvest. Being the only available protein, gorilla meat is as prized as sirloin is over here, and the village guest of honor was served a choice cut. Proudly, a platter of the usual mashed yam was placed before her — but with a roast gorilla hand thrusting artfully up from the center.

Is there any polite way out besides the back door?

Most experienced business travelers say no, at least not before taking at least a few bites. It helps, though, to slice whatever the item is very thin. This way, you minimize the texture — gristly, slimy, etc. — and the reminder of whence it came. Or, "Swallow it quickly," as one traveler recommends. "I still can't tell you what sheep's eyeballs taste like." As for dealing with taste, the old canard that "it tastes just like chicken" is often mercifully true. Even when the "it" is rodent, snake — or gorilla.

Another useful dodge is not knowing what you are eating. What's for dinner? Don't ask. Avoid poking around in the kitchen or looking at English-language menus. Your host will be flattered that you are following his lead, and who knows? Maybe it really *is* chicken in that stew.

9

Will you pasta the test?

In Europe, the hazard is not so much exotica as richness, amplitude, and hour. In Italy and Spain (as well as in Latin America), lunch is the biggest meal of the day and can last two or three hours. Work nevertheless is expected to continue afterward. Because Latins are used to this regimen — and wisely eat a very light breakfast and late-late supper — it does not mean the rest of us can take on a seven-course lunch, con vino, and survive a 4:30 meeting. If food is served family style from communal dishes, take just a little of everything. When ordering from the menu, ask for appetizer portions instead of entrée size, especially of the heavier pasta dishes. In French restaurants, request that, if possible, sauces be served on the side. In Scandinavia, do not try matching your host's trips around the smorgasbord herring for herring. Another trick is to order two appetizers, the second appetizer becoming your entrée; that way you eat sparingly but are politely eating in pace with your hosts.

Speaking of fish, in Japan it is often served raw. Nearly every meal begins with it and some restaurants serve nothing but. Although sushi bars may be just as trendy here as there, many Americans still find raw *any*thing literally tough going.

Sushi (a circle of raw fish packed artfully in rice) and sashimi (same thing without rice) are a problem for the uninitiated because they cannot be cut into small bites — it is all in one gulp or nothing. But there is usually red caviar sushi and sometimes Japanese vegetables can be substituted. One worldly Swiss who thought he had seen — and eaten — just about everything in the Orient describes, not so fondly, how he temporarily lost his taste for fish there. At a lavish Tokyo restaurant, delicacy after delicacy had been served. Then the pièce de résistance. A live fish was brought flopping and gasping to the table, and was delicately sliced by the maitre d' and served a piece at a time.

How to say no in Chinese

In Chinese cultures (Taiwan, Hong Kong, and Singapore as well as the mainland), the trick is to say it with*out* saying it. An endless history of famine and deprivation has made it bad manners for the host not to keep filling your dish — and for you not to keep eating as long as your dish is full. Obviously, a no-win situation.

(Incidentally, it is not rude for the Chinese to use the chopsticks they eat with to serve you.)

Eat what you are offered.

One way to discourage refills is to keep your rice bowl close to your mouth until you are done. Then lay your chopsticks across the bowl to signify "enough!" However, you will probably have more than one dish, thus undermining the effectiveness of the chopstick ploy. Same for your teacup, which seems to be magically replenishing itself no matter how much you drink. To stop the flow, leave your cup full. To say thank you, rap your fingertips lightly on the table. And always leave some food in your dish to indicate that your host was so generous you could not possibly finish.

Shark's fin soup is often the highlight of a Chinese multi-course dinner, served somewhere in the middle, and — incidentally — the polite time for toast making. Also, the second-to-last course is often plain boiled rice — which you should refuse! To eat it signifies you are still hungry and is an insult to the host.

Menus by Dostoevsky

When it is dinnertime in the USSR, the first thing you notice is that hotel and restaurant doormen are not there to help you *in* but to keep you *out*, at least until they determine that you really are a tourist. (Ordinary Russian citizens are not allowed into the same restaurants and shops to which aparatchiks and foreigners have access.) So don't wait for a welcoming smile and an open door. Whip out your visa and hope the doorman is in a good mood.

At lunchtime, it is not unusual to find restaurants closed to *every*one, even the commissars. The help, you see, are out to lunch. But even when they are on the job, there will be a classic Russian wait — as long as two hours before a waiter or waitress gives you a sidelong glance. Be consoled, though. You always have at your table two large bottles — one of mineral water, the other of hundred-proof vodka. Provided you can still read by the time the waiter gets there, you will find the menu an adventure all its own. "Every Continental dish ever served from St. Petersburg to Sicily is listed," reports a New Yorker back from Moscow. With a red plush cover, golden tassels, and nearly as many words as *War and Peace*, this is Stakhanovite austerity?

In theory, no. But then you order. Nyet. Nyet. Nyet. That is your waiter advising you that they do not have that tonight . . . or that . . . or that. Until you give up and ask what they *do* have. The answer varies. In some restaurants it is fish, in others chicken. So you turn to page 42 of your menu, marked chicken. More nyets. Okay, *which* chicken? Chicken Kiev, of course. Henry Ford, who promised to give American consumers any color car they wanted as long as it was black, would have approved.

And then there are Bolshevik breakfasts, alas not designed to appease appetites weaned on flapjacks and sunnysides. The usual choice is compressed fish (a layer cake of whatever turns up in the net, flash-frozen and then more or less thawed) and/or hard-boiled eggs. One visitor exultantly discovered a big, juicy Danish pastry in his hotel cafeteria one morning on his last trip. It took just one bite to reveal that it was more Russian than Danish, however, being stuffed with raw cabbage.

Table Talk

THANK YOU'S*		TOASTS*
Shay-shay	Mandarin	Kam-*pay*
Doe-jay	Cantonese	Yum-*sing*
Arr-i-*gah*-toe	Japanese	Kam-*pai*
Shu-kran	Arabic	No alcohol, no toast
Grah-see-as	Spanish	Sah-*lood*
Ohb-ri-*gah*-toe	Portuguese	Sah-*ude*
Grahtz-ee	Italian	Sah-*loo*-tay
Mare-*see*	French	Ah-votre-sahn-*tay*
Dahnk-ah	German	*Pro*-zit
Tak	Scandinavian	Skoal
Spa-*see*-bah	Russian	Nah-zda-*roe*-vee-ah

*Phonetic spellings

Also, while Americans answer a "thank-you" with a "you're welcome," the English don't. They answer a "thank-you" with a "thank-you."

Bottoms up — or down?

Some countries seem to do it deliberately, some inadvertently, except for Islam, where they don't do it at all. Either way, getting visitors as tipsy as possible as fast as possible stands as a universal sign of hospitality, and refusal to play your part equals rebuff. Wherever you go, toasts are as reciprocal as handshakes: if one does, all do. "I don't drink, thank you" rarely gets you off gracefully. Neither does protesting that you must get up early. (So must everyone else.)

"I try to wangle a glass of wine instead of the local firewater," one itinerant American says. "The only trouble is, the wine is usually stronger than the hard stuff." Mao-tai, Chinese wine made from sorghum, is notorious for leaving the unsuspecting thoroughly shanghaied. The Georgian wine so popular in Russia is no ladylike little Chablis either. In Nordic lands, proper form for the toast is to raise the glass in a sweeping arc from belt buckle to lips while locking stares with your host. It takes very few akvavit-with-beer-chasers before you both start seeing northern lights.

In Africa, where all the new countries were once old European colonies, it is often taken for granted that if you are white you must have whiskey or gin or whatever the colonials used to like. A traveler to a former French possession describes the dilemma of being served a large gourdful of Johnnie Walker Red at nine in the morning. The host was simply remembering how the French had always loved their Scotch. *When* they drank it and *how much* were details he had never noticed. Yet there was no saying no without giving offense. A few sips had to be taken and a promise made to finish the rest later.

Basic Rule #3: Clothes can also *unmake* the man.

Black tie, green tails. It was a very proper black tie affair in Australia's capital of Canberra. In a sea of ebony dinner jackets and starchy white shirtfronts bobbed a small riot of color — namely, the U.S. ambassador clad in dazzling pea-green sports coat and multihued plaid trousers. Why, the ambassador's wife asked plaintively, do these Aussies gape at us every time we show up at one of their fancy-dress receptions?

Wherever you are, what you wear among strangers should not look strange to *them*. Which does not mean "when in Morocco wear djellabas," etc. It means wear what you look natural in — and know how to wear — that also fits in with your surroundings.

For example, a woman dressed in a tailored suit, even with high heels and flowery blouse, looks startlingly masculine in a country full of diaphanous saris. More appropriate, then, is a silky, loose-fitting dress in a bright color — as opposed to blue serge or banker's gray.

In downtown Nairobi, a safari jacket looks as out of place as in London. With a few exceptions (where the weather is just too steamy for it), the general rule everywhere is that for business, for eating out, even for visiting people at home, you should be very buttoned up: conservative suit and tie for men, dress or skirt-suit for women. To be left in the closet until you go on an outdoor sightseeing trek:

- jeans, however haute couture
- jogging shoes
- tennis and T-shirts
- shorts
- tight-fitting sweaters (women)
- open-to-the-navel shirts (men)
- funny hats (either)

Where you *can* loosen up, it is best to do it the way the indigenes do. In the Philippines, men wear the *barong* — a loose, frilly, usually white or cream-colored shirt with tails out, no jacket or tie. In tropical Latin American countries, the counterpart to the barong is called a *guayabera* and, except for formal occasions, is acceptable business attire. In Indonesia, they wear *batiks* — brightly patterned shirts that go tieless and jacketless everywhere. In Thailand, the same is true for the collarless Thai silk shirt. In Japan, dress is at least as formal as in Europe (dark suit and tie for a man, business suit or tailored dress for a woman) except at country inns (called *ryokans*), where even big-city corporations sometimes hold meetings. Here, you are expected to wear a kimono. Not to daytime meetings but to dinner, no matter how formal. (Don't worry — the inn always provides the kimono.)

One thing you notice wherever you go is that polyester is the mark of the tourist. The less drip-dry you are, the more you look as if you have come to do serious business, even if it means multiple dry-cleaning bills along the way.

Take it off or put it on — depending

What you do or do not wear can be worse than bad taste — ranging from insulting to unhygienic to positively sinful. Shoes are among the biggest offenders in the East, even if you wear a 5AAA. They are forbidden within Muslim mosques and Buddhist temples. Never wear them into Japanese homes or restaurants unless the owner insists, and in Indian and Indonesian homes, if the host goes shoeless, do likewise. And wherever you take your shoes off, remember to place them neatly together facing the door you came in. This is particularly important in Japan.

(Note: The torture of sitting for hours cross-legged on tatami mats has been alleviated lately in some Japanese restaurants, which have thoughtfully cut a hole in the floor under the table so Westerners can unfold their legs.)

In certain conservative Arab countries, the price for wearing the wrong thing can hurt more than feelings. Mullahs have been known to give a sharp whack with their walking sticks to any woman whom they consider immodestly dressed. Even at American-style hotels there, do not wear shorts, skirts above the knee, sleeveless blouses, or low necklines — much less a bikini at the pool.

Basic Rule #4: American spoken here. You hope.

It is nice to be born free. But we should be just as grateful that we were also born speaking the language more people speak besides their own than any other. Even where Americans aren't understood, *American* is. It is when we try to talk in other tongues that the most dramatic failures of communication seem to occur.

At a party in Bernardsville, New Jersey. A high-level U.S. communications man invited a group of visiting Taiwanese that he had met in Taiwan to a reception at his house. He also invited some neighbors, one of whom had the bright idea of asking her laundryman how to say hello in Chinese. He gave her the words — but not the warning that every Chinese word has many meanings, depending on the tone you use. As the first Taiwanese came in the door, she delivered a smart "How do you do?" in Chinese. Bewildered, the guest turned to the host and demanded, "Why is this woman talking about my mother?" The word to indicate a question also means horse and scold and sesame seed — and mother. A case of wrong tone, wrong meaning.

At a banquet in Peking. As the honored guests at one of China's famous twelve-course governmental dinners, a delegation of heavy-duty equipment manufacturers from the Midwest had just laid down their chopsticks. It was time for a word, in quickly memorized phonetic Chinese, from our side. "Thank you very much for the dinner. I am so full I must loosen my belt" is the toast the Americans had prepared. But through the vagaries of the language what was actually delivered was, "The girth of thy donkey's saddle is loose." Again, good thought, bad pronunciation.

Sometimes the way we speak is as misinterpreted as what we are trying to say. Take the "conversation tango" we are accused of dancing with Latins. Most of us prefer to keep our distance in casual conversation — two or three feet apart when face to face. Nearly every South American, however, feels positively lonely at such a remove. He immediately tries to establish intimacy and intensity by virtually nose-to-nosing it with you. You take a step back, he takes a step forward. Back . . . forward . . . back . . . forward. Cha cha cha. Trouble is, the net impression can be: 1) you are a snob or 2) he is not nice to be near. The embarrassment to both sides is not worth demanding your territorial rights. So, stand your ground and let him stand his.

English English

"England and America," George Bernard Shaw said, "are divided by a common language." To an American on London's Carnaby Street, English English can sound as foreign as Brooklynese to a member of the House of Lords.

Fridge, loo, telly, wireless, and chemist's are all easy enough to decipher. But who would suspect that a bonnet is a car hood, a vest an undershirt, a panda a police car, a counter jumper a salesman — or fanny an X-rated word (use bum instead)? Should you run into a serious cockney, one who drops his aitches and substitutes rhyming phrases for words (trouble-and-strife for wife), you may as well be talking in Minsk.

Belgium has two official languages, Dutch and French, and the character of the country changes with the language. Around Antwerp (where there are mostly Flemish and hence Dutch), you find more order and efficiency in the way things get done. Around Brussels (where there are mostly Walloons and hence French), you find more three-star restaurants. A nice contrast, either way.

Speaking geography

In Scotland, the only *Scotch* is what you drink. The people are called *Scots*. Tartans, terriers, and the language itself are *Scottish*. Never use the three interchangeably.

In the Middle East, it is equally *lingua non grata* to refer to the Persian Gulf. Over there, it is always the Arabian Gulf. Nor are Muslims ever called Muhammadans. Better not say Russia to a Russian. Post-revolutionary tact demands USSR. To East Germans, their land is the GDR (for German Democratic Republic) and East Berlin is plain Berlin. Whereas in West Germany, it is just as verboten to leave the East or West off either Germany or Berlin.

Never-never land

It is a basic precept of Japanese culture that the best face must be put on even the worst situation — which sounds comforting but can have confusing consequences. For a Westerner given to firm yes's and no's, either it *is* a deal or it isn't. For his Japanese counterpart, a smile, a nod, even a spoken affirmative can simply be reluctance to disappoint — especially in front of others.

Ask the man in charge for an answer to your business proposition and not only will he be offended but his answer will be meaningless. Those details are expected to have been disposed of at a lower level, privately, between subalterns.

Unfortunately, when you are asking a cabdriver if he understands where you want to go, there is no one else to answer for him. Nine times out of ten he will indicate "you bet!" and step on the gas. Many visitors to the Ginza have, as a result, found themselves in Osaka. One man of the world thought he had solved the problem. When leaving his hotel, he would have the concierge write out his destination in Japanese characters. For his return, he would simply take a hotel matchbook and flash it at the driver. Late one night, he discovered that the matchbook has its drawbacks.

As usual, the driver took one look and zoomed purposefully off. The ride had begun to seem unusually long, however, and downtown Tokyo was nowhere in sight when the cab stopped. All was empty streets and darkened warehouses. The driver had taken him not to the Okura Hotel but to the matchbook factory.

If you ever do hear a no in Japan, from either cabdriver or captain of industry, it is likely to be not so much a word as a sucking of breath through the teeth that comes out sounding like "sah." Otherwise the closest anyone comes is to say sadly, "It is very difficult."

Tread softly and carry a dictionary

Some languages cannot be understood as pronounced by outsiders. But no matter how you twist most native tongues some meaning gets through — or at least you get an *A* for effort if it doesn't. Memorizing a toast or greeting (in spite of the tales above) nearly always serves to break the ice, if not the communications barrier.

Even in France, where abusing the language is as punishable as stomping the tricolor, you find that to take out a French-English dictionary nearly always draws a crowd avid to help you unravel the mysteries of how to say, "Where is the Metro, please?"

But no matter how fluently the natives speak your language, remember that it is never spoken — nor understood — quite the same way it is at home. Steer clear of all slanguage, from colloquialisms to curses to down-home references that have about as much resonance in Paris or Peking as grits and chitlins.

This is especially true if you are reaching your audience through a translator. Deliberately or not, what *he* is telling them may not be what *you* are telling them. One company spokesman from Wisconsin, using an interpreter at an overseas press conference, found that his message had been completely misunderstood. Not through mischief, but because the interpreter had added a touch of glamor and newsworthiness to what struck him as deadly dull business talk. Whenever possible, have another bilingual there to monitor the translation for you so you know what you really said.

George Washington? Who's he?

That is no way for a foreigner to win friends in Washington. Nor is arriving on someone else's doorstep knowing nothing of the government, economics, religion, history, or national character of the place the way for an American to hit a home run. Yet those harried business trips with their if-it's-Tuesday-this-must-be-Zagreb itineraries can leave anyone speechless.

If you can possibly schedule a lunch with a couple of people who have lived or done a lot of business where you are going, it will be well worth the price of a filet of sole. Also, grab the last few issues of a newsmagazine if your destination is often in the news. This way, even if you do not have any real background on it, you will at least be able to discuss what happened there last week.

If your company has a library, you can get a cram course right out of the files. Or, if you have branches in the places where you are headed, write ahead asking for a briefing. Whatever you get in return will at least be enough to start asking intelligent questions when you get there. Instead of "Mobuto? Who's he?"

Talking business

When you *don't* talk business can be as important as when you *do*. In Britain, for instance, as soon as the day is done, so is business, and nothing will turn your hosts off faster than continuing shoptalk over drinks and dinner.

On the other hand, to the Japanese there is almost no distinction between the business day and the business night. They consider it part of both their personal and professional lives to spend virtually every evening with business associates. Not at the office but at bars, nightclubs, geisha houses, and private clubs. Whether business is or is not discussed, the purpose is nonetheless business. "You get through to a man's soul at night" is a saying among Japanese businessmen. No matter how many mornings you have ended the business day at 4 A.M., begging off is bad form.

One time when you do *not* talk business in Japan, though, is at the beginning of first meetings. Introductions call for a set ritual. Business cards are exchanged. Tea is poured. And then more tea is poured. And still more. However anxious you are to get started, this is a not-to-be-rushed first step that the Japanese use to digest not just the tea but who you are, where you fit into your company's pecking order, and how your status relates to their status. This information about you is passed among those present — as well as to people not even in the room — so your counterparts can agree precisely on how to deal with you.

The same slow, analytical start often occurs in Arab countries, too. But with an added dimension: the multiple meeting. While conducting business with you in his office, the man in charge is very likely talking to a stream of other people wandering in and out. You may be dropped in midsentence and not picked up again for twenty minutes. No disrespect is meant; this is the communal "family style" in which Middle Eastern business is done. Do not be surprised, then, when a meeting you thought would take an hour takes two or three. And do not go over someone's head because you think there is a faster way to get a quick decision. It has the opposite effect.

Religion and Sex: Protocol at its Pinnacle

If discussing politics is like playing with matches, transgressions in the areas of religion and sex are like playing with live hand grenades. Still, neither area can be ignored. Religion is often an important part of a culture (e.g., the Middle East) and therefore an unavoidable adjunct to business or tourist travel. For Westerners, who are usually Christian-oriented, a respectful — repeat, respectful — conversation about some of the other great religions of the world can be both illuminating and ingratiating.

As for sex, while Americans are slowly learning to change their vocabulary from *businessman* to *businessperson*, that change is not occurring as rapidly outside the U.S. In most other countries, *business* is still largely synonymous with *men*.

Thus, both subjects should be dealt with head-on. Here goes.

Where religion is a religion

When a prosperous international advertising agency opened an office in Bangkok, the manager was warned it would never succeed. But why not? All the agency's other Far Eastern branches were having great success. "Ah," it was explained, "you never put yourself above Buddha before!" (A prominent statue of the god was, in fact, one flight below the new office and just across the street.) After a year there, business was still zero. In spite of himself, the manager decided to be philosophical about it and moved the office to where there was no Buddha, and business has been thriving ever since.

All Buddhist images, even the famous tourist sites, are holy and never to be photographed without permission. Other Thai sensitivities lurk where you would never expect to find them. Door sills must never be stepped on, for Thais believe that kindly spirits dwell below. But to open a window at night is to let evil spirits in. And to touch the head of even a close friend risks ending the friendship, so sacred do they consider the head.

In Hong Kong, the key word is *joss* which, loosely translated, means good luck, but is more akin to a blessing.

In Muslim countries, proper dress and proper decorum between the sexes are as important as observing any civil laws. It is no mere quaint local custom to stop everything five times a day for prayers. While you are not expected to kneel or face Mecca, you must let those who do do — without interruption or impatience. Whenever it can be done gracefully, making a religious gesture toward an Arab is the sincerest form of flattery. It can be as simple as saying *Inshallah*, which means "God willing" and is used as commonly as "okay" is here. As in "See you tomorrow, *Inshallah*" or "When does your flight leave, *Inshallah*?" It is easy to pick up the habit — and a nice compliment to your host.

Also remember that every culture has its own holidays, which are considered truly *holy days*. To schedule a business trip during Ramadan, Carnival in Rio, Chinese New Year, etc., is like a foreigner's asking you to attend a meeting on Christmas morning. For the holidays and their dates, contact the consulate or tourist bureau or check with a travel agent.

In the battle of the sexes, America is still way ahead

From mailrooms to boardrooms, women are becoming as commonplace in American corridors of power as button-downs and wing tips. Here but not there. Around most of the world, it is the same old *Vive la différence*.

Don't photograph religious images.

In Britain and Western Europe, a few women have risen — or are rising — through the ranks. Nevertheless, at every level above bookkeeper and clerk you will be dealing with a solid phalanx of homburgs and bowlers. Usually, there is no awkwardness when a Ms. VIP sits down at the conference table. And she will suffer no embarrassment eating alone in restaurants or even stopping off for a drink at a pub or bistro. (The latter is not quite so true, though, in Spain, Portugal, Southern Italy, and Greece.)

The farther east you go, the tougher the going gets. A New York banker reports that just half a dozen years ago she was refused a visa to parts of the Middle East on the grounds that she was both a woman and single. Even today, women are forbidden to drive cars or ride bicycles in Saudi Arabia.

Another American, invited to the wedding party for the daughter of a close Arab friend, discovered that separate is equal but still very separate. The party was actually *two* parties at two different hotels, each with exactly the same banquet and exactly the same festivities. The only difference was that one was for the bride and all the female guests, while the other was for the groom and all the male guests. Never the twain did meet.

Even if an Arab invites you home, his wife (or wives) will probably not be seen (although she may well be in the kitchen supervising dinner). It is not polite to inquire about her (them), and if you do meet, be warm but undemonstrative. Do not even shake hands unless she takes the initiative, which she no doubt will not. On the other hand, when that same Arab businessman comes to your country, his wife just may accompany him and then she should receive all the courtesies of any Western woman.

Whether you are a man or a woman, it is advisable to mention your family life as assurance of your stability as a business associate. In Eastern cultures, family ties are extremely important, and for those who come from a less family-oriented part of the world, it does not hurt to refer to hearth and home. Of course, replays of Little League games and snapshots of the barbecue and the hamster can put anyone to sleep.

Sorry, ladies — no wrestling or geishas

The one place of business in Japan where women can be found in large numbers and at high levels is the geisha house. Ironically, women guests are not welcome, however. (Not because geisha houses are bordellos. They are not. But because the "girls" consider it their territory.) When a U.S. financial manager insisted his wife accompany him, she received a stern lecture from the English-speaking geisha at their table. The American, she said, was "a good woman, clever with children" and therefore belonged at home with them — not out on the town, sipping sake and listening to samisen music.

In case you might be feeling athletic, two other men-only spots in Japan are sumo wrestling rings and certain mountains considered too sacred to be climbed by women, who are also forbidden to touch Buddhist priests or even hand them anything except through an intermediary (male, of course).

Lecturer and writer Anna Chennault, a business consultant on the Orient, declared, "Chinese women do not worry about liberation. They have been liberated because of necessity." Perhaps, but few women are noticeable in the upper reaches of the People's Republic's officialdom, although they do comprise 60 percent of the labor force. But in the Philippines, women seem to be in charge of many things. Filipino families educate their daughters in U.S. universities — and not necessarily to be wives, but also bankers and lawyers.

Women also have a very strong role in Africa, both in the home and in business. Yet visitors should remember that in Muslim — and Buddhist — nations, the religious stricture against mixing the sexes socially still obtains. A woman traveling as chief emissary for her Fortune 500 corporation was surprised after meeting with men all day to be placed at a table with their wives at dinner. The wife of the chairman emeritus of a multinational advertising agency has found this to be an advantage. After countless tours of her husband's worldwide advertising empire, she says she learns more about the country *and* the company from the wives. Their eye for detail, their slight remove from office politics, and their candor bring a different perspective to the conversation. And when an office manager won't admit to a problem or to a daring new idea often his wife will admit it for him.

In Latin America as well, women are smoothly accepted into business and governmental hierarchies. But in a land where machismo is every man's birthright, it does not pay to come on like Superwoman.

At presentations, sales meetings, even in personal conversations — particularly when the woman speaking outranks any men present — it is useful to avoid a lot of "I did's" and "I know's" in favor of "At our company, we found that . . ." or "We approach the problem this way . . . ." Not bad advice for men, either.

After-hours Etiquette

Never risk losing your credentials as a serious businesswoman by what you do *after* business. In Western European countries, this is almost never an issue. But elsewhere it is easy to raise eyebrows — and lower your prestige. It isn't so much what you actually do as what it *looks* as if you might do.

1. Avoid eating or drinking alone in restaurants that the locals or business travelers use to pick up women. This usually includes most European-style restaurants and hotel dining rooms. Room service, of course, is an alternative. And so is safety in numbers: invite a few of the women in the office where you are doing business to join you (on *your* expense account, naturally).

2. Unless it comes from your company, do not give male colleagues any but the most perfunctory gift unless obviously earmarked for the home or children.

3. If you are (or were) married, use a Mrs. even if you don't at home.

4. Make it a point to mention your husband and children (if you have any), and also ask about your male counterpart's family. If the question of dinner arises, invite them, too.

5. As soon as you are introduced to the family, stop talking business and strike up a rapport with the others.

6. In Latin countries, men make overt approaches whether they know you or not. Just returning a look on the street can give you problems. With business acquaintances, a firm if unflattering no is often more diplomatic than playing it coy or ambiguous.

7. Above all, do not date anyone you are there to do business with. If he is irresistible, wait until he comes over here.

On Your Best Behavior

In the world of cultural behavior, the only truly safe generalization is: don't generalize.

"All Americans are loud and lacking in grace." "The English are cold and aloof." "The French are romantic but often rude." So it goes. And each generalization can be blasted and disproven.

Still, there are some general rules about each region and each nation. Each rule will have its exception, but an awareness of the rules places you in an advantageous and more comfortable position.

In the area of protocol, here is a potpourri of general advice.

In EUROPE, the general rule of thumb is to behave as if you were calling on a rich old auntie. While the New World may have loosened up dramatically in the past couple of generations, the Old one remains very buttoned up — literally and figuratively. What would be mildly bad manners at home (gum chewing, talking with hands in pockets, legs propped up on furniture, backslapping, etc.) are cardinal sins in Continental company. Suit coats stay on in offices and restaurants and on the street, even in July. Women do not wear pants to work or to dressy restaurants. First names are never used without invitation and that usually only comes after long association. Those with academic titles and degrees expect you to use them as a sign of respect. Except in Southern and Eastern Europe, the handshake serves as standard greeting but is executed with a much limper squeeze and with no American-style arm pumping and shoulder thwacking. For all business introductions and most personal ones, an exchange of business cards is de rigueur. Smoking at the table is frowned on until cognac and coffee are served. Punctuality is a must.

In France, they are appalled by the way anyone else speaks French — including some other Frenchmen. Unless you are urged to trot out your Berlitz lessons, it is safer to stick to English except for greetings, toasts, and an occasional isolated phrase. Be prepared to field argument, criticism, and controversial subjects such as California wine vs. French, why soccer is superior to football, etc. The French are proud of their education (much more rigorous than most Americans') and their opinions — and relish showing off both in feisty debate. They get right down to business matters but are slow to come to decisions, displaying a seemingly endless fascination with minute details. Whether the decision is good news or bad, they state their intentions unambiguously. Haute cuisine, of course, is no laughing matter, and you must pay proper respect to what is on your plate at even the most perfunctory business lunch. Many French people are offended by dinner guests who begin a meal with palate-numbing drinks like martinis and Scotch.

In Germany, gentlemen walk and sit to the left of all ladies and men of senior business rank. Men rise when a woman leaves or returns to the table. Your dinner guest will expect you to have made arrangements in advance and not show up asking, "Got any ideas where we should eat?" Formality and punctiliousness are more pronounced here than anywhere else in Europe, possibly the world. One mistake to avoid at all costs is mixing up West Germany's official name (the Federal Republic of Germany) with East Germany's (the German Democratic Republic).

In Great Britain, it isn't so much what you do as how you do it. The British public school (what we call private or prep school) specializes in manners and self-discipline. In business, emotions are rarely vented and protocol is given the utmost attention. However, business is kept firmly in its place (the office), while lunch, dinner, and weekends are strictly for socializing. Be sure to issue *your* invitations well in advance. The British keep engagement calendars as religiously as Boswell kept his diaries, and get-togethers are booked days — even weeks — in advance. If you get an invitation reading "black tie" or "smoking," it means men must wear dinner jackets with all the proper accompaniments from studs to black silk hose and women must wear long dresses. Renting formal wear is blessedly simple in London. Moss Bros. (pronounced as one word: "mossbros") is famous for renting (the British call it hiring) all forms of formal wear. At formal dinners, the host sometimes says Grace. This is a signal that after the main course the Loyal Toast will probably be offered. This is a toast to Her Majesty's health, and after that you may smoke — *but never before*. By and large, dinner at 7:30 means at 7:30. You may be ten minutes late but not ten minutes early. It is not customary to take gifts unless there is a special reason: a birthday, anniversary, or reciprocation for a gift received. The usual practice is to take flowers. If the value of the gift exceeds fifteen dollars or so, it may cause embarrassment.

Quiz: Know the difference between England, Britain, and the United Kingdom? (Most visitors don't.) England, Scotland, and Wales comprise Great Britain and when Northern Ireland is added, it becomes the United Kingdom.

Not only is British dress conservative but so is the conversation. Unlike the French, Britons prefer less controversial chitchat than politics and religion usually provide. The safest subject, particularly in England, is animals, for whether they shoot them or let them sleep in the parlor, the Queen's loyal subjects are unashamed lovers of fur, feather, and fin. It is noteworthy that in England there is a *National* Society for the Prevention of Cruelty to Children but a *Royal* Society for the Prevention of Cruelty to Animals.

Most honorary (as opposed to hereditary) titles such as Sir, Dame, and Lord are used even among familiar acquaintances. Before addressing such a person by name, it is wise to hear how others do it.

In pubs, the change you leave on the counter for your next drink may be taken as a tip by the bartender, so keep it in your pocket until you are ready to reorder. If you want Bourbon, ask for it that way, because "whiskey" means Scotch. When pulling out a cigarette, always offer them to your "mates." Reason: cigarettes are, and always have been, very expensive in England. But it is also just a polite custom.

Avoid striped ties in case they are copies of British regimentals, for one does not wear an old-school tie when one has not attended the old school.

Keep in mind that many "English" words have a totally different meaning from their American usage. For example: *lift* (elevator), *chemist* (druggist), *vet* (a verb meaning to examine critically or appraise), and *intercourse* (a friendly dialogue as in, "I had intercourse with the taxi driver all the way to Picadilly").

Elsewhere in Europe, observing the national differences between countries that, to us, perhaps seem nearly indistinguishable is very important. Austrians appreciate being recognized for their own character and accomplishments (Mozart was *not* a German) and although not the case in Germany, it is always polite in Austria to greet people in public, even complete strangers. In Belgium, the Flemish and the Walloons are as different as the Dutch and the French (whence they came) and should be treated with similar distinctions; the Flemish, incidentally, kiss cheeks *three* times, alternating cheeks.

In Bulgaria, a nod means no and a shake of the head means yes.

In both Denmark and Sweden, the toast can be a very formal regimen. You must never toast your host or anyone senior to you in rank or age until they toast you, nor must you touch your drink until the host has said *skoal*. If you are seated at your hostess's left, you should propose a toast to her during dessert; if on her right, you are expected to make a short speech of appreciation.

In Greece, there are no rules of greeting; they may shake hands, embrace, and/or kiss at the first and every meeting. Punctuality is not a must.

Iceland is the exception to the rule of not calling people by their first names. It is, in fact, impolite to use *last* names. Making definite appointments and getting there on time are simply not done.

In Italy, handshaking is a national pastime, but seldom do Italians remember names on first introduction. All university graduates have a title and usually expect you to use it (*dottore* for liberal arts, *avvocato* for law, *ingegnere* for technical fields, and *professore* for both professors and most medical doctors).

In the Netherlands, the toast is given just before and just after the first sip. Punctuality is a must.

In Spain, the only time you must take punctuality seriously is when attending a bullfight. Most offices and shops close for siesta all the way from 1:30 to 4:30 P.M., and restaurants do not usually reopen until after 9 or get into full swing until 11.

In Switzerland, needless to say, punctuality is a way of life (and don't complain that your watch, which is almost certainly Swiss, is slow).

In the FAR EAST, countries that are side by side are often as different as Nome and Honolulu. Indeed, no other continent has a greater variety of languages, races, and religions, and these often shape a nation's character more profoundly than any national border. Once you have crossed the Pacific, stop generalizing — except in one particular. Politeness. It is the one transcending trait shared by all Asiatics. Diffidence between individuals and harmony among the group take precedence over any personal feelings or ambitions that may be kicking and screaming inside your head.

In Japan, they never say no in public, which is why American businessmen often take away the wrong impression. But this obsession with pleasing does not mean that the Japanese make quick friends, particularly with Western businesspeople. A rollicking night out on the town will not necessarily lead to signing the contract to your advantage the next morning. *Naniwabushi* (to get on such close personal terms with someone that he will have to do you a favor) is standard Japanese operating procedure. Hence, accepting lavish gifts from a Japanese business acquaintance can lead to obligations that may later prove awkward, if not downright painful.

The People's Republic of China is the latest incarnation of the world's oldest civilization, one whose social and cultural achievements were, for centuries, the most sophisticated on earth. While visitors cannot help arriving with their own political and cultural baggage, it is polite to remember that the Chinese, too, have a very strong sense of self — of their own value system and their own style. Once known as "the giant with the tiny appetite," China more and more seeks the same economic goals as the rest of the world — but often with methods true to its most ancient traditions. The age-old obsession with keeping face is still alive and well there.

You see it in their concern with who goes through the door or sits down first. (Always let *them* have the right-of-way.)

You see it in their sensitivity to status and title. (Never rely on "Mr." to take the place of a person's proper title, such as "Committee Member" Wang, "General" Li, "Factory Manager" Hsieh, or "Bureau Chief" Chang. Also, never call anyone "Comrade" unless you are one yourself.)

And, most often, you see it in their painfully cautious deliberations in business matters. (As one Western sales representative says, "The same transaction that would take a week in New York, two in Paris, and three in Rio may take months in Peking. And then a year after they've said yes or no they can change their minds.")

The Chinese are superb hosts, masters of the twelve-course banquet and frequent dinner toasts. No drink but beer should be touched until a toast is proposed. This is sometimes done with a long, elaborate speech or sometimes by merely raising the glass and making eye contact. Only a symbolic sip need be taken in reply.

Chinese frequently show regard for a member of their own sex by publicly holding hands or by some other physical contact, but the opposite sexes rarely make any public show of affection. Great respect is shown to older people, and punctuality is a given.

Elsewhere in the Far East, where the Chinese culture has been exported by centuries of Chinese expatriates, expect to find much the same preoccupation with maintaining one's self-esteem. Putting a good face on even the worst situation remains a way of life even in Hong Kong and Singapore, where the English have introduced an equal dose of Westernization. Visitors are often pleasantly surprised by the serendipity of East meeting West. For example, both New Years are commonly celebrated. And while politeness and mutual respect are never given short shrift, business deals are handled with a crisp efficiency Lord Keynes might have applauded.

Just because the Chinese dominate a culture, however, it does not mean that other influences will not be encountered. In Malaysia, for instance, you will be given chopsticks and a spoon when dining with a Chinese, but if your host is a Hindu or Malay you may get nothing at all (your hands are your utensils for the evening). Pork, of course, is a staple of Chinese cooking, but Malays will not touch it. On the other hand, Hindus and Buddhists avoid beef. Buddhists are also extremely sensitive to being touched on the head, especially in Thailand.

While the handshake takes precedence over any other greeting in most Oriental countries (except Japan), Thais still prefer the *wai* (pronounced why), which is executed by placing both hands together in a praying position at the chest. The higher the hands, the more respect you show, although eye level is the highest anyone goes. Do not ever make light of either Buddha or the Royal Family to a Thai, for God and King are taken with ultraseriousness. There is never any touching between the sexes (even married ones) in public, and that includes dancing. So, if you hear a waltz, stay seated. Don't be surprised to be called by your first name at first meeting as in Mr. Bob or Miss Jennifer: Thais use first names in even the most formal circumstances. When shopping in Thailand, remember that except in department stores and bookstores, prices are merely an invitation to bargain and may be anywhere from 100 to 300 percent higher than the seller is willing to accept after vigorous haggling.

In India, East and West meet again in a simmering stew of contrary customs. The host who says "How do you do?" in impeccable Oxford English may nonetheless greet you with a reverential *namaste* (palms together and a nod of the head). Muslim women are kept from the view of men outside their families, and even non-Muslim women seldom show up at social functions or sit at the dinner table or join in the conversation even in their own homes. (That red dot on forehead or hair usually means a woman is married.) You will find most Indians equally well informed on love potions, magic charms, and soothsaying as they are on the international scene.

In the USSR, there is no Oriental-style masking of emotions and keeping your cool. Expansiveness, generosity, and letting go are everything. Stingy is one of the worst epithets you can hurl at a Russian. All things Western, from jeans to rock 'n' roll, are idolized here. *Unofficially.* It is a serious crime for tourists to sell anything to Soviet citizens. It is also illegal to bring in dissident literature (to be on the safe side you'd better limit your carry-ons to Jack London and Mark Twain), to take out art objects, including religious artifacts, or to change money unofficially. The one rule you are free to break is no tipping — if you are subtle about it. To get there at all, plan your trip well in advance: it takes weeks, sometimes months, to arrange visas, guides, transportation within the country, and contacts with the necessary Soviet agencies.

The MIDDLE EAST no longer generates the mystery — or misgivings — for Western travelers that it did before "Come with me to the Casbah" became "Meet you in the conference room." Arabs are proud of their new place in the world economy and enjoy hearing outsiders acknowledge it. They also relish the facility with words which their oil-financed educations at Oxford, Yale, and the rest of the world's ivied halls have bestowed. However, to outsiders those words can be swords. Arab rhetoric and bombast, born of an ethnic tradition of high passions and short fuses that historians trace back centuries to pre-Islamic days, are not reserved for global enemies alone. An Arab is as quick to explode at friend as at foe. Not only is there no stigma attached to sounding off, but it is looked on as a handy safety valve — a first line of defense, or offense — that makes the ranter feel better without having done any real harm to the rantee.

The other side of the instant frown, however, is the instant smile. Arab preoccupation with both personal and public opinion can lead to misunderstandings. As Arab author Sania Hamady writes, "The desire to please — to pave the way for favorable and happy relationships with possible good results — may induce them to say what is agreeable without regard to truth." This, added to the habit of giving their word rather than their signature to agreements, can make an outsider believe he has a yes when the answer was really no.

Handshakes are the custom outside the home, but a host may welcome you with a kiss on both cheeks and you should reciprocate. Do not ask for an alcoholic drink unless it is offered, and do not bring the hostess a gift or inquire about her (she will almost certainly be kept out of sight and out of the conversation).

It is important to arrive at both social and business affairs on time. But do not expect to *leave* them on time. An Arab's sense of the world around him is that of an extended family, and he will interrupt even the most serious discussion to deal with whomever seeks his time and counsel. He will also stop all business several times a day to pray, either at the office or at the nearest mosque. No irritation should ever be shown at these digressions; they are an unshakable rule of Islamic life, writ not in sand but in stone.

No one expects you to speak Arabic, but a few words can be endearing to a people proud of their heritage and history. *Sahtein* is the equivalent of *bon appétit. Soufra daiman* means, roughly, "May food be always available on this table." You will probably have ample cause to use both, since Arabs are famous for their hospitality — and gargantuan banquets. Skip breakfast and lunch the day you are invited. Less likely is the opportunity to say *sahha* (cheers!), given the near nonexistence of strong drink in Islam. Pork and shellfish are also forbidden. Any animal that scavenges or has a cloven hoof is shunned by devout Moslems.

A shared cup of thick coffee or mint tea usually precedes any business dealings. Giving and taking are never done with the left hand. Ditto for eating. The business week runs from Saturday to Wednesday or Thursday, with Thursday and/or Friday the Muslim day of rest and worship. No work is done after noon during Ramadam, the ninth month of the Islamic lunar calendar.

In Saudi Arabia, greetings are particularly elaborate: first, you say *salaam alaykum;* second, you shake hands, accompanied by the words *kaif halak;* next, a Saudi will often extend his left hand to your right shoulder and kiss you on both cheeks. Thereafter, he is likely to take your hand in his, publicly or privately, as a show of kinship. (If you should be entertaining a Saudi over here, you will probably find that he realizes hand holding is taboo. In case he hasn't heard, however, you might want to mention it, making a slight joke of it.)

Remember, too, that in Saudi Arabia they go by lunar time: watches are set differently, days and months do not follow our Gregorian calendar, and the year is counted from Mohammad's death (about 622 A.D.).

In AFRICA, there is such a diversity of language, custom, and culture that few rules reach beyond national borders and practices can vary wildly within a nation, such as Nigeria, with clearly defined tribal areas.

In LATIN AMERICA, you can behave anyway you like, as long as you are simpatico — meaning that you must feel comfortable with Latin ways before Latins will feel comfortable with you. Those ways, to a newly arrived Northerner, can be very *unc*omfortable at first. Women are put off by the machismo, which runs the gamut from swaggering and flirting to taking for granted that any female over fifteen is available and no doubt willing, regardless of her marital status and his attractiveness. For men, it is the opposite side of the macho coin that causes problems. Emotions are much closer to the surface (some would say feminine) and are likely to boil over into tears, rapture, fury, or sentimentality with an ease at which most American men feel uneasy. Eye contact must be unflinching. Conversation must be nose to nose. Shoulders are squeezed. Lapels are fondled. Hugs and two-handed handshakes are common among mere acquaintances. Hospitality and generosity are carried to what many Americans consider a fault. Admire a Latin's new gold watch and he may give it to you.

Siesta and *mañana* are two words that set many Americans' teeth on edge — the former because it means that just about everything, including stores, banks, and business offices, closes for two or three hours in early afternoon, and the latter because it means that things get done when they get done and people get there when they get there. In fact, there is a positive revulsion toward being the first to arrive. To "blend with the crowd," it is customary to arrive at least a quarter of an hour late and in busy traffic-jammed cities like Mexico City, it is more like an hour or even two.

It is hard to know at first meeting if a Latin identifies more with his Spanish or his Indian heritage. Better to let him reveal his sentiments before waxing poetic about one or the other, lest it be taken as a slight to the preferred blood line.

Another practice that requires advance information is haggling over prices. It varies from country to country (yes in Mexico, no in Chile) and from shop to shop.

AUSTRALIA, although it can take 26 hours on a jet to get there, is as close to home as many Americans ever feel away from home. A wry Englishman visiting Chicago described it as "instant Australia." Unlike most other people who shared in World War II with us, the Australians have never forgotten it and remember warmly how the Yanks helped win the day on both sides of the world. It may be the only place on earth where American servicemen do not immediately jump into civilian clothes when off duty. There is nothing an Australian likes better than to chat it up with a stranger at a pub. Most visitors report that it is impossible to have a lonely, morose drink by themselves, unless, of course they are female.

The surprise on this friendly, classless continent is that liberation has not reached the "second" sex yet. Here, macho does not mean ogling and innuendo. It simply designates a mateyness among men on which no woman dare intrude. One commodity of which there is none is British reticence. One handshake or beer and you are on a first-name basis. When it comes to punctuality, probably none but the Germans take it more seriously, but otherwise the Aussies are as unbuttoned and easygoing as any good ol' boy at a catfish fry.

CHAPTER 2

Hand Gestures
and
Body Language

A Risky Language
or
Actions speak louder than words — and often say all the wrong things

"I knew I'd committed a monumental goof. But I just couldn't imagine how."

A young computer salesman from New Jersey is remembering his first overseas sales pitch. The scene was his company's offices in Rio, and it had gone like a Sunday preacher's favorite sermon. As he looked around the table, he knew he had clinched the sale. Triumphantly, he raised his hand to his Latin customers and flashed the classic American okay sign — thumb and forefinger forming a circle, other fingers pointing up.

The sunny Brazilian atmosphere suddenly felt like a deep freeze. Stony silence. Icy stares. Plus embarrassed smirks from his colleagues.

Calling for a break, they took him outside the conference room and explained. Our hero had just treated everyone to a gesture with roughly the same meaning over there as the notorious third-finger sign conveys so vividly here. Apologies saved the sale, but he still turns as pink as a Brazilian sunset when retelling the tale.

It is only natural when you find yourself at sea in the local language to use gestures to bail yourself out. Anyway, even when you can be understood, isn't it friendlier and more endearing to say it with a hand, an eye, or some other intentional body language? Yes. But only if you know what the sign is really saying. Gestures pack the power to punctuate, to dramatize, to speak a more colorful language than mere words. Yet, like the computer salesman, you may discover that those innocent winks and well-meaning nods are anything but universal.

Ever since World War II, V has meant victory all over the world. Even Winston Churchill, however, was very careful how he used it. For in Britain, unless your palm is facing outward — toward your audience — the V sign is the equivalent of the third finger.

How Men Around the World React
to Seeing a Pretty Girl

- The American lifts his eyebrows.
- The Italian presses his forefinger into his cheek and rotates it.
- The Greek strokes his cheek.
- The Brazilian puts an imaginary telescope to his eye.
- The Frenchman kisses his fingertips.
- The Arab grasps his beard.

Be prepared for incoming messages, too

On his maiden trip to the Middle East, a Midwestern public relations man stepped from the cool of an ultramodern conference center into the dust and glare of an ancient roadway. Donkey carts rustled up whirlwinds of stinging sand. The air rang with a mullah's bullhorned call to prayer. Without a word, a Saudi who had attended the same conference reached down and gently took his hand. The word exotic was taking on new meaning, and the meaning set off a panic button in the visitor's brain. "What does this Arab think . . . ?" "What will all the *other* Arabs think . . . ?" Etc., etc. Finally, common sense set in. Of course, the gesture was just a simple signal of trust: silent Arabic for friendship and respect.

Even unconscious gestures can be unsettling to the uninitiated. Just back from a tour of several Arabian Gulf countries, a woman recalls how jumpy she felt talking to men there. "Not because of what they said," she explains, "but what they did with their eyes." Instead of the occasional blink, Arabs lower their lids so slowly and languorously that she was convinced they were falling asleep.

In Japan, eye contact is a key to the way you feel about someone. And the less of it, the better. What a Westerner considers an honest look in the eye, the Oriental takes as a lack of respect and a personal affront. Even when shaking hands or bowing — and especially when conversing — only an occasional glance into the other person's face is considered polite. The rest of the time great attention should be paid to fingertips, desk tops, and the warp and woof of the carpet.

"Always keep your shoes shined in Tokyo," advises an electronics representative who has logged many hours there. "You can bet a lot of Japanese you meet will have their eyes on them."

On the other hand (or foot), Arabs flinch at the sight of shoe soles. Hence, feet are best kept flat on the floor — never propped up on a table or desk or crossed over the knee.

Bye-bye no-no

In Europe, the correct form for waving hello and goodbye is palm out, hand and arm stationary, fingers wagging up and down. The common American wave with the whole hand in motion means no — except in Greece, where it is an insult that is likely to get you into big trouble. In many countries, hitchhiking with a thumb stuck out is also a very rude gesture. However, it is easy for a traveler to lapse into old habits, in which case — as long as you are recognized as an American — the reaction will probably be nothing worse than a frown.

Please touch (sometimes)

Touching can be a very touchy business. In most Latin lands from Venezuela to Sicily, the *abrazo* (hug) is as commonplace as the handshake. Between men and men — and women and women. This is also true in Slavic countries, where it is better described as a bear hug. The French sometimes add a man-to-man peck on the cheek.

The Japanese, though, have an aversion to casual body contact. While most Japanese who come to the West make the concession of shaking hands, they remain more comfortable at home with the traditional bow from the waist. The proper form is with hands sliding down toward the knees or at the sides, back and neck stiff, and eyes averted.

Their democratic sensibilities quivering like whiskers on a catfish, many Americans regard bowing as out-and-out kowtowing. In Japan, where there is nothing demeaning or obsequious about it, the bow remains the time-honored way of saying, "I respect your experience and wisdom." When in doubt, do it anyway. It works.

For the casual encounter, one brief all-purpose bow will fill the bill. But on formal occasions — a high-level business meeting, say — the true Oriental bow with all its delicate gradations may turn out to be the only medium you and your opposite number have with which to

41

communicate. A Wall Street investment banker and veteran of countless American-Japanese conferences explains why.

"For us Westerners," he points out, "it's risky to try enunciating anything more complicated than 'sayonara.' As for the Japanese executive, the more senior he is, the less likely he is to understand English — he has an army of ambitious underlings to understand it for him. His seniority also means he has not come to the meeting to do business — those decisions have already been made at a lower level."

So why is he there at all? "Mainly, to see who it is he's doing business *with*." Hence, on these occasions form is frequently more telling than content.

With business inferiors: Always allow them to bow lower and longer than you do.

With equals: Match bows, adding an extra one when you want to show a slight edge of respect, as with someone substantially older than you or with a customer whose business you are trying to get.

When unsure of status: The safest move is to bow a shade less low than the other person.

With the top man: If he clearly outranks you, make sure you out-bow him even if it takes your knuckles all the way to the floor. Also, remember to keep your eyes respectfully lowered. Which, of course, isn't easy when you are trying to see how low *he* is bowing to *you*.

And, in Japan never bow with a hand — or both hands — in your pockets. In fact, never shake hands or give a speech with hand-in-pocket.

Learn all this and you'll become a Laurence Olivier in the art of bowing.

International Gesture Dictionary

Gestures Using the Face

Eyebrow Raise: In Tonga, a gesture meaning "yes" or "I agree." In Peru, means "money" or "Pay me."

Blink: In Taiwan, blinking the eyes at someone is considered impolite.

Wink: Winking at women, even to express friendship, is considered improper in Australia.

Eyelid Pull: In Europe and some Latin American countries, means "Be alert" or "I am alert."

Ear Flick: In Italy, signifies that a nearby gentleman is effeminate.

Ear Grasp: Grasping one's ears is a sign of repentance or sincerity in India. A similar gesture in Brazil — holding the lobe of one's ear between thumb and forefinger — signifies appreciation.

Nose Circle: The classic American "okay" sign — the fingers circle — is placed over the nose in Colombia to signify that the person in question is homosexual.

Nose Tap: In Britain, secrecy or confidentiality. In Italy, a friendly warning.

Nose Thumb: One of Europe's most widely known gestures, signifying mockery. May be done double-handed for greater effect.

Nose Wiggle: In Puerto Rico, "What's going on?"

Cheek Screw: Primarily an Italian gesture of praise.

Cheek Stroke: In Greece, Italy, and Spain, means "attractive." In Yugoslavia, "success." Elsewhere, it can mean "ill" or "thin."

43

Fingertips Kiss: Common throughout Europe, particularly in Latin countries (and in Latin America). Connotes "aah, beautiful!," the object of which may be anything from a woman or a wine to a Ferrari or a soccer play. Origin probably dates to the custom of ancient Greeks and Romans who, when entering and leaving the temple, threw a kiss toward sacred objects such as statues and altars.

Chin Flick: "Not interested," "Buzz off," in Italy. In Brazil and Paraguay, "I don't know."

Head Circle: In most European and some Latin American countries, a circular motion of the finger around the ear means "crazy." In the Netherlands, it means someone has a telephone call.

Head Nod: In Bulgaria and Greece, signifies "no." In most other countries, "yes."

Head Screw: In Germany, a strong symbol meaning "You're crazy." Often used by drivers on the autobahn to comment on the driving skills of other travelers, this gesture can get you arrested! The same gesture is used in Argentina, but without the consequences.

Head Tap: In Argentina and Peru, "I'm thinking" or "Think." Elsewhere it can mean "He's crazy."

Head Tilt: In Paraguay, tilting the head backward means "I forgot."

Head Toss: In Southern Italy, Malta, Greece, and Tunisia, a negation. In Germany and Scandinavia, a beckoning motion. In India, "yes." Unfamiliar elsewhere.

Hand and Arm Gestures

Horizontal Horns: A gesture of self-protection against evil spirits in most European countries. In some African countries, a variation — pointing the index and third finger toward someone — can be interpreted as putting the "evil eye" on him. Use with discretion.

Vertical Horns: In Italy, signifies that you are being cuckolded. But in Brazil and other parts of Latin America, can be a sign of good luck.

V Sign: In most of Europe, means victory when, as Churchill did, you keep your palm facing away from you. Margaret Thatcher has been known to forget this — and to get roundly hooted for it, for the same gesture palm *in* means, roughly, "Shove it." In non-British-oriented countries, it generally means two of something as in "Two more beers, please." It was, by the way, not an Englishman but a Belgian who first made the V synonymous with victory in World War II.

Beckon: To use finger(s) to call someone is insulting to most Middle and Far Easterners. It is proper in most of these countries, and in Portugal, Spain, and Latin America, to beckon someone with palm down, fingers or whole hand waving.

Fingers Circle: Widely accepted as the American "okay" sign, except in Brazil, where it's considered vulgar or obscene. The gesture is also considered impolite in Greece and the USSR, while in Japan, it signifies "money," and in southern France, "zero" or "worthless."

Fingers Cross: In Europe, crossed fingers have several meanings, most commonly "protection" or "good luck." In Paraguay, the gesture may be offensive.

Fingers Snap: In France and Belgium, snapping the fingers of both hands has a vulgar meaning. In Brazil, it connotes something done long ago or for a long time.

One-Finger Point: In most Middle and Far Eastern countries, pointing with the index finger is considered impolite. The open hand is used instead, or, in Indonesia, the thumb.

Two-Finger Tap: In Egypt, this means a couple is sleeping together and, true or false, is always rude. Can also mean, "Would you like to sleep together?"

Third-Finger Thrust: Not nice in any language, this old favorite has survived for more than 2,000 years. (The Romans called the third finger the "impudent" finger.)

Third-Finger Reverse: Same meaning as executed by an Arab.

Fist Slap: "——— you" in Italy, Chile, and many other places.

Forearm Jerk: Another way of saying the above or some variation thereof, especially in Mediterranean countries.

In England, however, it connotes a sexual compliment, equivalent to a wolf whistle.

Thumbs Up: In Australia, a rude gesture; in almost every other place in the world, simply means "okay."

Flat-Hand Flick: The universal flicking of the fingers toward the source of irritation, meaning "Go away" or "Get lost."

Palm Push: In Nigeria, pushing the palm of the hand forward with fingers spread is a vulgar gesture.

Hand Pat: In Holland, "He/she is gay."

Hand Purse: Can signify a question or good or fear. Considered almost the national gesture of Italy.

Hand Saw: When you make a deal in Colombia and intend to share the profits, the gesture is: one palm facing down with the other hand making a sawing motion across the back of the hand facing down.

Hand Sweep: In Latin America and the Netherlands, a sweeping or grabbing motion made toward your body, as though you were sweeping chips off a table, means that someone is stealing or "getting away with something." The same gesture in Peru means "money" or "Pay me."

Waving: Called the *moutza* in Greece, this is a serious insult, and the closer the hand to the other person's face, the more threatening it is considered. Same in Nigeria. Never use it to get a waiter's or cabdriver's attention. In Europe, raise the palm outward and wag the fingers in unison to wave "goodbye." Waving the whole hand back and forth can signify "no," while in Peru, that gesture means, "Come here."

Height: In Colombia and much of Latin America, only an animal's height is indicated by using the whole hand, palm down. It is polite to hold the palm facing the

observer to show human height, or, in Mexico, to use the index finger.

The Wai: Traditional greeting in Thailand. Called the *namaste* in India.

Arms Fold: In Finland, folded arms are a sign of arrogance and pride. In Fiji, the gesture shows disrespect.

Elbow Tap: In Holland, "He's unreliable." In Colombia, "You are stingy."

The Fig: In some European and Mediterranean countries, an obscene gesture of contempt. In Brazil and Venezuela, a symbol of good luck reproduced in such diverse forms as paper weights and golden amulets worn around the neck.

47

A Quick Guide
to the
Ways of the World

This section has been compiled in an effort to provide the fast-moving international business executive — as well as the casual tourist — with a quick, helpful reference list. Countries are grouped by regions of the world, and are arranged alphabetically within groups. For more details on a specific country, refer to the Index.

Europe

Here are some general tips that the traveler will want to remember when visiting European countries.

General Protocol
What would be mildly bad manners at home (gum chewing, talking with hands in pockets, legs propped up on furniture, back slapping, etc.) are cardinal sins in Continental company.

Names/Greetings
First names are never used without invitation and that usually comes only after long association. Those with academic titles and degrees expect you to use them as a sign of respect.

Except in Southern and Eastern Europe, the handshake serves as standard greeting but is executed with a much limper squeeze and with no American-style arm pumping and shoulder thwacking.

For all business introductions and most personal ones, an exchange of business cards is de riguer.

Appointments/Punctuality
Punctuality is a must, especially in Northern European countries.

Hospitality/Gift Giving
Smoking at the table is usually frowned on until cognac and coffee are served.

Sending flowers is a safe and appreciated gift gesture.

Dress
Suit coats stay on in offices, restaurants, and on the street.

Women do not wear pants to work or to dressy restaurants.

Austria

General Protocol
Austrians appreciate being recognized for their own character and accomplishments, and although not the case in Germany, it is always polite here to greet people in public, even complete strangers.

Never call an Austrian a German. While they speak the same language, Austrians and Germans have distinct customs and different values.

Appointments/Punctuality
Arrange business appointments in advance and try to be punctual.

Hospitality/Gift Giving
Give flowers or some small gift such as chocolates when invited to a home for the first time for dinner or for a visit other than business.

Conversation
Avoid discussions about money, religion, or politics unless you are specifically asked about them.

Belgium and Luxembourg

General Protocol
Privacy is a jealously guarded right and is carefully respected.

Names/Greetings
In Belgium cheek kissing is done three times, alternating cheeks. Do not be surprised to see men embracing.

It is customary to greet and say goodbye to each person at a social or business gathering with a handshake.

Appointments/Punctuality
Punctuality is very important.

Hospitality/Gift Giving
Avoid sending a gift of chrysanthemums. They are a reminder of death.

Conversation
Politics, local language differences (French-Flemish), and religion are generally topics to be avoided. The Belgians will often tell jokes about the Dutch — and vice versa. Better to stay out of that regional rivalry.

Bulgaria

Names/Greetings
Since you are in a Communist country, address a man or woman as "Comrade" with the last name.

Appointments/Punctuality
Make business appointments far in advance. Be punctual.

Hospitality/Gift Giving
If you are invited to a home, take flowers, candy, or wine.

Conversation
Avoid discussing politics and social conditions in Bulgaria.

Gestures
A nod means "no" and a shake of the head means "yes."

Czechoslovakia

General Protocol
Avoid taking photographs in museums or art galleries. Do not photograph military installations, airports, policemen, or soldiers.

Appointments/Punctuality
Make business appointments far in advance. Be punctual.

Hospitality/Gift Giving
If you are invited to a home, take flowers, wine, whiskey, or cognac.

Conversation
Avoid discussing politics and social conditions. A good topic of conversation: sports.

Denmark

General Protocol
No taxi tipping. Shake hands — both men's and women's.

Like all Scandinavians, Danes love the summer months. It's difficult — and inconsiderate — to conduct heavy business in July and August. And in some Danish beach resorts, don't be surprised to see topless bathing suits, and maybe even less.

Appointments/Punctuality
Punctuality is a must.

Hospitality/Gift Giving
Toasting with a *skoal* is common — directly to an individual or to the whole crowd.

Danes like to surprise others with their potent aquavit (literally, "water of life"). So be forewarned.

A bouquet of flowers taken to the home will always be well received.

Men might consider packing a tuxedo because senior businessmen stage more black-tie dinners than in other countries.

East Germany

General Protocol
Their land is the GDR (for German Democratic Republic). And East Berlin is plain Berlin.

Before visiting an industrial plant, a foreign businessman must have a permit issued by the Ministry of Foreign Trade.

Appointments/Punctuality
Appointments are essential. However, businesses do not accept appointments on Wednesday.

Hospitality/Gift Giving
Take flowers when you are invited to a meal and present them unwrapped. Avoid roses. They have romantic implications.

Conversation
Show courtesy to all party officials and avoid political discussions.

England, Scotland, and Wales

General Protocol
In business, emotions are rarely vented and protocol is given the utmost attention. However, you may find the Welsh and Scots more informal.

Avoid the word "English." You'll please everyone if you use the word "British."

The *Scotch* is what you drink. The people are called *Scots* or *Scotsmen*. Tartans, terriers, and the language itself are *Scottish*.

Names/Greetings
Most honorary titles are used even among familiar acquaintances. But it is wise to first hear how others address a person.

Appointments/Punctuality
Appointments are essential. You may be ten minutes late, but not ten minutes early.

Hospitality/Gift Giving
As soon as the day is done, so is business, and nothing turns your hosts off faster than continuing shop talk over drinks and dinner.

Invitations to people's homes are much more forthcoming than in most Northern European countries. Be sure to issue *your* invitations well in advance.

An invitation reading "black tie" or "smoking" means men must wear dinner jackets with all the proper accompaniments from studs to black silk hose and women must wear long dresses.

Businessmen are not usually invited home for dinner, as most business entertaining is done in pubs and restaurants. However, should you be invited to dinner at a British home, flowers and chocolates would be a suitable gift to the lady of the house on arrival. Avoid white lilies. They suggest death.

You may smoke after the toast to Her Majesty's health, but *never* before.

Entertainment in the form of lunch, dinner, drinks, or a night at the theater or ballet usually takes the place of gift giving.

The noon meal is usually the main meal of the day.

Dress
Avoid striped ties in case they are copies of British regimentals.

Conversation
What not to talk about: politics, gossip about the monarchy, and religion. Avoid starting a conversation with "What do you do?" That's considered rather personal.

Gestures
Ever since World War II, the V sign has meant victory all over the world. But be sure your palm is facing outward — toward your audience.

Finland

General Protocol
No taxi tipping.

Remember that Finland is very different from the other three countries generally lumped together as "Scandinavia."

Names/Greetings
Stay your distance — no Russian-type bear hugs at greetings.

Appointments/Punctuality
Appointments should be made well in advance. Be punctual.

Hospitality/Gift Giving
If you are invited to a Finnish home for dinner, take some flowers for the hostess.

Alcohol is often consumed in great quantities and varieties at dinners so be wary if unaccustomed to heavy drinking.

Although Finns are not formal people, a toast generally is drunk at the beginning of a meal. In addition to dinner, guests may be invited to take a sauna with the host, but mixed gender saunas are not common.

Conversation
Avoid discussions of religion or politics.

France

General Protocol
French businessmen tend to be rather formal and conservative.

Natives are appalled by the way anyone else speaks French —
including some other Frenchmen.

Appointments/Punctuality
Prior appointments are the rule. Punctuality is a sign of courtesy.

Hospitality/Gift Giving
An invitation to visit someone's home, even after long acquaintance, is rare. But for that occasion, a small gift of flowers or chocolates for the hostess will be appreciated.

Cuisine, and therefore noon and evening meals, are an important and respected part of daily life.

Gifts that appeal to intellect or aesthetics are especially appreciated. Avoid gifts with large, prominent stamps of your company name.

Conversation
Avoid personal questions, politics, and money as topics of conversation.

Greece

General Protocol
The elderly are respected, addressed by courteous titles, served first, and have much authority.

Names/Greetings
There are no rules for greeting. They may shake hands, embrace, and/or kiss at the first and every meeting.

Appointments/Punctuality
Punctuality is not a must.

While prior appointments are not usually necessary, the courtesy of phoning ahead will be appreciated.

Hospitality/Gift Giving
Greek hospitality is sincere, incredibly generous, and sometimes overwhelming. Be careful not to praise a specific object, or the host may insist on giving it to you.

If you are invited to a Greek home, take flowers or a cake for the hostess.

In Western Europe, logo gifts should be
in good taste and unobtrusive.

Conversation
Topics to avoid in conversation: Cyprus and other controversial aspects of international politics closely affecting Greece.

Gestures
A slight upward nod of the head means "no," *not* "yes."

A Greek may smile only when happy, but sometimes he will smile when very angry.

Hungary

General Protocol
Do not photograph soldiers or military installations.

Do not bring antisocialist printed matter or a hunting weapon into the country.

Hospitality/Gift Giving
If you are invited to dinner at home, take Western liquor or wrapped flowers as a gift.

Conversation
Good topics of conversation: food, wine, what you like about Hungary. Avoid discussing politics or religion.

Iceland

General Protocol
Tipping is an insult.

Names/Greetings
Here it is impolite to use an Icelander's *last* name. So, you should call them by their first names.

Appointments/Punctuality
Punctuality is not a must.

Business appointments are not usually necessary, as a tradition of "dropping in" prevails.

Hospitality/Gift Giving
It is common to take a small gift to the host or hostess when you are invited to a meal.

Ireland

Appointments/Punctuality
Make business appointments in advance, but keep in mind that the Irish are not very time conscious.

Hospitality/Gift Giving
If you are invited to an Irish home, a gift of flowers or chocolates for the hostess will be appreciated.

If you are invited to dinner, good gifts include a bottle of wine, flowers, chocolates, or cheese.

Giving business gifts is not a common practice.

Conversation
Avoid discussion of religion or politics.

Israel

General Protocol
Remember, Israel is surrounded by Arab countries, and customs, in most cases, are completely different.

The Sabbath (Saturday) is strictly observed by Orthodox Jews from nightfall on Friday to nightfall on Saturday.

Names/Greetings
Shalom is the usual greeting.

Titles are even less important in Israel than in the U.S.

Appointments/Punctuality
Even though Israelis in general are casual about time, you should be punctual.

Prior appointments are necessary.

Hospitality/Gift Giving
An invitation to visit should be responded to by setting a time, date, and place.

A gift of a book is an excellent choice since most Israelis are eager readers.

Conversation
Subjects to avoid in conversation: religion and the large amount of U.S. aid that has helped the country to survive.

Italy

Names/Greetings
Handshaking and gesturing are national pastimes.

All university graduates have a title and usually expect you to use it.

Appointments/Punctuality
Make business appointments well in advance.

Punctuality is not an Italian virtue — at least for social events.

Hospitality/Gift Giving
Lunch is the biggest meal of the day and lasts two or three hours.

To refuse a very insistent invitation to lunch or dinner is considered ungracious. If the occasion takes place at home, you should take wine, flowers, or chocolates. Avoid taking chrysanthemums, which are only used for funerals. Take an odd number of flowers.

The exchange of business gifts is quite common in Italy.

Conversation
Common topics for discussion include politics, soccer, family affairs, business, and local news.

Topics to avoid in conversation: American football and politics.

The Netherlands

General Protocol
Do not tip your taxi driver.

Appointments/Punctuality
Prior appointments are expected, as is punctuality.

Hospitality/Gift Giving
It is customary to give flowers, chocolates, or something similar as a gift. Gifts that are novel and new are appreciated. They should be gift wrapped. Do not include food as a gift.

A toast is given just before and just after the first sip.

Conversation
The Dutch people appreciate compliments on their furniture, artwork, carpeting, and other home furnishings.

Conversation topics to avoid: American politics, money, and prices.

Good topics to discuss: Dutch politics, travel, and sports.

Norway

Appointments/Punctuality
Norwegian businessmen are strong on punctuality and precision. Should you be unable to keep an appointment, cancel or postpone it by phone.

Avoid business trips to Norway in July, August, and early September — winters are long, and the sun is the visitor they enjoy most during those months.

Hospitality/Gift Giving
If invited to a Norwegian home, bring a small gift of flowers or chocolates for the hostess.

Laws in Norway are harsh about drunken driving, so in social gatherings, one person may be designated as the driver — and that person abstains from alcohol.

Conversation
Personal topics such as employment, salary, and social status usually are avoided.

Good topics of conversation include hobbies, politics, sports, and travel.

Poland

Appointments/Punctuality
Prior appointments are absolutely necessary.

The economy is largely state-owned and operated, so expect frequent appointments and delays in decisions.

Hospitality/Gift Giving
It is customary to take flowers for the hostess for even a brief visit. They should be handed to the hostess unwrapped. A word of caution: red roses denote romantic love.

Toasting is often a part of both formal and informal dinners.

Consumption of hard liquor is widespread in Poland and you may well be plied with cognac at business and other meetings.

Conversation
Don't refer to German or Russian involvement in World War II.

Good topics of conversation include Poland and its cultural history, life in the U.S., and your family and its activities.

Portugal

Names/Greetings
It is the custom in Portugal for men to greet each other with the *abraço* (embrace) — an enthusiastic hugging and mutual slapping of backs. For women, a kiss on both cheeks is customary among close acquaintances.

Appointments/Punctuality
Businessmen should avoid making appointments between noon and three o'clock in the afternoon when everything closes down.

While Portuguese do not stress punctuality, the visitor should be prompt. Prior appointments are absolutely necessary.

Hospitality/Gift Giving
You are not obliged to take a gift if you are invited to dinner. Instead, return the favor by taking your hosts to a restaurant.

Conversation
A visitor should avoid discussing politics and government. It is polite to converse about the family, positive aspects of Portugal, and personal interests.

Romania

Appointments/Punctuality
Prior appointments are necessary. Romanians are very punctual, so be on time.

Hospitality/Gift Giving
If invited to a Romanian home, which is rare, don't forget flowers for the hostess.

Gifts for your host's family could include perfume, cosmetics, jeans, or coffee. Gifts for a businessman could include imprinted pens or lighters — of the inexpensive variety.

Conversation
Good topics of conversation include sports, travel, music, fashion, and books.

Avoid discussing politics, Russia, communism, or any negative aspects of Romania.

Spain

General Protocol
A break — the siesta — in the middle of the day allows families to be together for the main meal of the day. Most offices and stores are closed between 1:30 and 4:30 P.M.

Names/Greetings
Men who are close friends often give each other an *abrazo* (hug). Women friends greet and part with a slight embrace and a kiss on each cheek.

Appointments/Punctuality
The only time punctuality is taken seriously is when attending a bullfight.

Hospitality/Gift Giving
An oddity in Spain is the lateness at which people eat dinner. Restaurants do not generally open until after nine and do not get into full swing until about eleven.

You may take flowers when you are invited to dinner (avoid dahlias and chrysanthemums as they are associated with death). Other gifts could include pastries, cakes, and chocolates.

Conversation
Good topics of conversation include politics (but it is best to avoid political comparisons between Spain and the U.S.), sports, and travel.

Avoid discussions of religion, family, and job. Do not make negative remarks about bullfighting.

Sweden

General Protocol
Signs of thoughtfulness: knowledge of the cultural differences among Sweden, Norway, Denmark, and Finland; and awareness that the Swedes are more liberal socially and politically than the others.

Appointments/Punctuality
Punctuality is a must.

Hospitality/Gift Giving
A bouquet of flowers for the hostess will be appreciated.

Because of severe penalties for driving while intoxicated, one person in your social gathering will be designated driver, and will avoid alcohol.

Toasting can be more formal than in the other Scandinavian countries. For example, your Swedish hosts might be impressed if you were aware of these (somewhat old-fashioned) rules:

- Never toast your host or anyone senior to you in rank or age until they toast you.

- Don't touch your drink until the host has said *skoal.*

- To be very, very proper, the *skoal* motion is: move the glass from the waistline up to the eyes, look the other person directly in the eyes, say *skoal*, drink, make a wave of the glass toward your host's eyes, and bring it back down to the table.

Switzerland

Appointments/Punctuality
Appointments are essential and punctuality is highly valued.

Avoid making appointments during July and August — the vacation time.

Hospitality/Gift Giving
Impersonal gifts such as flowers or candy are in very good taste. Red roses, however, carry a romantic connotation.

Conversation
Good topics of conversation include sports, what you like about Switzerland, travel, and politics.

Topics to avoid: weight watching and diets (especially during meals), and questions about a person's age, job, family, or personal life.

Turkey

Appointments/Punctuality
Make appointments well in advance and be punctual.

Hospitality/Gift Giving
A Turkish businessman may invite you to his home, but he is more likely to take you to a restaurant for a leisurely evening.

If you are invited home for dinner, take flowers, candy, or pastries. If you know the family serves alcoholic beverages, you could take wine.

Conversation
Topics to avoid in conversation: politics, communism, and the Cyprus-Greece conflict.

Good topics for discussion: noncontroversial international affairs, families, professions, and hobbies.

Union of Soviet Socialist Republics

General Protocol
It is a serious crime for visitors to sell anything to Soviet citizens. It is also against the law to bring in dissident literature, to export art objects, or to change money with private citizens.

Refer to the country as the Soviet Union — not Russia.

Never drop anything — not even an old cinema ticket — in the street. It's both offensive to Russian tidiness and illegal.

Plan your trip to the Soviet Union well in advance. It will take weeks, perhaps months, to arrange visas, contacts with Soviet organizations, and travel details.

Names/Greetings
A Russian will shake hands and state his or her name when meeting someone for the first time. Greetings among friends often include hugging and kisses on the cheek.

Appointments/Punctuality
Be punctual for appointments.

Hospitality/Gift Giving
It is a common practice for guests to take flowers or liquor when invited to a Russian home. A gift of artwork or a book would be appreciated.

West Germany

General Protocol
It is verboten to leave the "East" or "West" off either Germany or Berlin.

Names/Greetings
Respect titles ("doktor") and *never* jump to a first-name basis until invited.
 Answer the phone by immediately saying your last name.

Appointments/Punctuality
Punctuality is essential. Should you be unable to keep an appointment, cancel it or postpone it by phone. Make appointments well in advance.

Hospitality/Gift Giving
Invitations into German homes are a special privilege. A man should bring flowers, which he will unwrap in the entrance hall and present to the hostess upon greeting her. Avoid red roses.
 A thank-you note should be sent within a few days for any hospitality.

Conversation
Avoid references to baseball, basketball, or American football in conversation. Instead, talk about the German countryside, hobbies, and such sports as soccer.

Yugoslavia

Appointments/Punctuality
Appointments are necessary, but try to avoid vacation time during July and August. Yugoslavs are generally punctual.

Hospitality/Gift Giving
Take flowers — an odd number but never thirteen — or wine to dinner. Chocolates, whiskey, or coffee beans are welcome gifts.

Conversation

Yugoslavs are more open in expressing political views than residents of other Communist countries. They are free to travel abroad and are accustomed to discussing government policies.

Good topics for discussion include lifestyles in the U.S., sports, family, and fashions.

Topics to avoid in conversation: religion and particularly sensitive political issues.

AFRICA

The African continent is divided into three distinct regions:

- The northern nations, bound together by language (Arabic), religion (Islamic or Moslem), and resources (oil). Incidentally, it is these shared elements that form the Arabic grouping; there is no such thing as an "Arabic" race or nationality.

- The black countries.

- South Africa.

Each of the countries of these three regions has distinct cultural characteristics, depending, of course, on its history and on the influence of the country that colonized it. As for general rules, the northern African nations follow Arabic protocol, gestures, etiquette, and behavior; the middle African nations are oriented to black multicultures; and South Africa is Dutch/English-oriented.

Algeria

Names/Greetings

Handshaking is common, both on meeting and leaving.

Visitors are always addressed by their title and last name. Professional titles are widely used.

Appointments/Punctuality

Prior appointments are recommended. Punctuality is not widely regarded.

Conversation

Topics to be avoided in conversation: politics and industrial problems.

Topics suitable for discussion: the increase in industrialization and agrarian reforms.

Egypt

General Protocol
The workweek runs from Saturday to Thursday. Friday is the Muslim day of rest.

Remember to remove your shoes before entering a mosque.

Hospitality/Gift Giving
Social engagements usually begin later than they do in the U.S. and dinner may not be served until 10:30 or later.

When invited to dine, it is customary to take a gift of flowers or chocolates. Giving and receiving gifts should be done with both hands or the right hand — never with the left.

When entertaining Egyptians, be sure to have some non-alcoholic drinks on hand.

Conversation
Subject to avoid in conversation: Middle Eastern politics.

Topics suitable for discussion: Egyptian advancement and achievement, the positive reputation of Egyptian leaders, Egyptian cotton, and their ancient civilization.

Ghana

General Protocol
Because of the wide degree of difference among the ethnic groups, it is difficult to describe any particular custom that is practiced all over the country.

Names/Greetings
It is customary to shake hands when meeting people and when leaving.

Appointments/Punctuality
Make appointments well in advance and be punctual, although Ghanians may be late or may not show up at all.

Ivory Coast

Names/Greetings
Handshaking is customary.

Appointments/Punctuality
Make appointments well in advance and be punctual, but do not be surprised if the host is not so particular.

Hospitality/Gift Giving
As for gifts, a product of your country — for instance, an imprinted or engraved ballpoint pen — would be welcome.

Conversation
Topics to be avoided: politics and lack of efficiency in some industries.

Subjects suitable for conversation include the successful economic achievements of the country and interest in the local culture.

Kenya

General Protocol
The British call it "Keenya," but the more proper pronunciation is "Ken-ya," after the modern-day founder, Jomo Kenyatta.

After English, Swahili is the language most common, and the word for "hello" is the delightful-sounding *jambo*.

If you have a new product to sell, you are advised to call on the chief purchasing officer of the Ministry of Works.

Names/Greetings
It is customary to shake hands when meeting people and when leaving.

Appointments/Punctuality
Prior appointments are necessary.

Conversation
Subjects to avoid in conversation: local politics and the Mau Mau period of the 1950s.

Libya

General Protocol
The economy is almost wholly state-controlled.

A traveler should be aware of current regulations on health, visas, currency, and commercial and security matters.

Appointments/Punctuality
Make appointments well in advance and be punctual, but there is little regard for keeping a schedule in Libya.

Hospitality/Gift Giving
Hospitality will generally involve invitations to meals or receptions. There are strict laws on the prohibition of alcohol.

If you are invited to a Libyan home for dinner, only men will be present. Take a gift for the host, but not for his wife.

Conversation
Topics to avoid in conversation: politics, religion, and other controversial subjects.

Morocco

General Protocol
You should offer to remove your shoes before entering a Moroccan home, and you always should remove them when you enter a mosque.

Names/Greetings
Shaking hands is customary.

Appointments/Punctuality
Prior appointments are advisable although punctuality is seldom observed.

Hospitality/Gift Giving
Moroccan businessmen will invite you to their homes for huge feasts, but you will rarely meet their wives.

Mozambique

Names/Greetings
First names are rarely used. Professional titles should be used if known.

Nigeria

General Protocol
Because of the wide range of customs and cultures among the ethnic peoples of Nigeria, a large variety of life-styles prevails.

Appointments/Punctuality
Nigerians understand the Western habit of punctuality, although they generally are not too concerned about time.

Prior appointments are important, especially with government officials. Be punctual.

Because travel within Nigeria is difficult, allow plenty of time to reach your destination.

Conversation
Topics to avoid in conversation include politics — particularly African politics.

Subjects suitable for discussion include their industrial achievements and plans for future development.

Senegal

Names/Greetings
It is customary to shake hands when introduced.

Appointments/Punctuality
Prior appointments are advisable.

While punctuality is recommended, do not be surprised if your host is a bit late.

Hospitality/Gift Giving
Never eat food with the left hand as this is considered offensive in the largely Muslim culture.

Conversation
Topics to be avoided: politics, government leaders, and religion.

Subjects suitable for discussion include the achievements of the country and its culture.

South Africa

General Protocol
South Africa is the industrial giant of Africa. It leads the world in the production of gold, diamonds, platinum, and antimony.

There are very strict conventions and social rules in South Africa regarding race and color. Best to follow the lead of your host in regard to these particular areas.

Appointments/Punctuality
Prior appointments are necessary, and punctuality is strictly observed.

Conversation
South Africa is one of the few countries where it is difficult to avoid discussion of local politics and especially the policy of apartheid. And you will find residents divided on the subject.

Most South Africans are bilingual, speaking English and Afrikaans (of Dutch origin).

Tanzania

Names/Greetings
It is customary to shake hands when being introduced.

Hospitality/Gift Giving
Gifts are often given by hosts at the time of departure from the country. At the same time, visitors may reciprocate by presenting their hosts with a gift.

Conversation
Topics for discussion include the Tanzanian National Parks, African culture, and international politics.

Subjects to be avoided in conversation include the prevailing political climate.

Uganda

Names/Greetings
Handshaking is common.

Appointments/Punctuality
Prior appointments are advisable. However, Ugandans may arrive late.

Hospitality/Gift Giving
If you are invited to someone's home, take along a gift for your host or hostess. Wives are automatically included in invitations unless it is specified otherwise.

Conversation
Most topics can be discussed freely. World affairs and the arts are among the most popular topics.

Zambia

Names/Greetings
Handshaking is common. Use courtesy titles or, if known, professional titles.

Appointments/Punctuality
A prior appointment is advisable although it is no guarantee that the meeting will take place.

Hospitality/Gift Giving
Gifts should not be offered to government officials. Employees of state corporations may be embarrassed if offered an expensive item. Small gifts, perhaps bearing an imprint of your company, would be welcome.

Conversation
Avoid discussion of the shortage of items in the shops, local politics, or any inefficiencies you may have noted in the country.
Zambians like to discuss international politics.

The Middle East

Here are some general tips that the traveler will want to remember when visiting the countries of the Middle East.

General Protocol

Proper dress and proper decorum between the sexes are as important as observing any civil laws.

Local Islamic religious custom demands everything stop five times a day for prayers. While you are not expected to kneel or face Mecca, you must not interrupt or display impatience when your host does.

Whenever it is done gracefully, making a religious gesture toward an Arab is the sincerest form of flattery. It can be as simple as saying *Inshallah*, which means "God willing" and is used as commonly as "okay" is here.

Remember to respect Ramadan (the ninth month of the Islamic calendar). No work is done after noon during Ramadan.

Do not refer to the Persian Gulf. There it's the Arabian Gulf.

Muslims are never called Muhammadans.

It is an insult to sit in such a way as to face your host with the soles of your shoes showing. Do not place your feet on a desk, table, or chair.

Names/Greetings

Handshakes are customary outside the home, but a host may welcome you with a kiss on both cheeks and you should reciprocate.

Take an adequate supply of business cards. It may be appropriate to have one side printed in English and the other in the local language.

Appointments/Punctuality

The business week runs from Saturday to Thursday, with Thursday and/or Friday the Muslim day of rest and worship.

Punctuality is important for the visitor although the host may not be on time.

Hospitality/Gift Giving

Even if an Arab invites you home, his wife (or wives) will probably not be seen (although she may well be in the kitchen supervising dinner). It is not polite to inquire about her (them), and if you do meet, be warm but undemonstrative. Do not even shake hands unless she takes the initiative, which she no doubt will not.

Do not ask for alcoholic drinks.

Pork meat and pigs are banned.

Be prepared to eat with your fingers if you see your host doing so. Eat with the right hand only.

Most entertaining is with other men and wives are seldom seen.

Writing instruments make excellent gifts. People of the Middle East like the look of gold and they prefer fountain pens for the grace and flow of their alphabet.

Conversation
Avoid talk about your pet dog back home.

Religion and politics are to be avoided in conversation.

It is safe to talk about the growth and development of the country visited.

The Gulf States

The Gulf countries comprise Bahrain, Kuwait, Sultanate of Oman, Qatar, and United Arab Emirates.

General Protocol
If an Arab businessman takes your hand and holds it as you walk, don't be alarmed. He means it only as a sign of friendship.

Names/Greetings
The customary greeting is: first, say *salaam alaykum*; next, shake hands while saying *kaif halak*; then, your host may place his left hand on your right shoulder and kiss you on both cheeks.

Appointments/Punctuality
Punctuality is important in Gulf countries.

While you must make prior appointments, don't be surprised to find several other businesspeople present and several meetings taking place at once.

Hospitality/Gift Giving
Skip a meal before dining at the home of an Arab businessman, so that you may show proper appreciation of the meal by eating copiously.

Your Arab host is likely to be very magnanimous. Be careful not to admire one of his possessions too warmly; he may insist on giving it to you, and you may be forced to accept rather than offend.

Gifts are appreciated but not expected. Avoid gifts of liquor and other items, such as photos and sculptures of women, that are prohibited by Islam.

Conversation
Topics of particular interest in these countries are falcons and horses. Avoid conversations concerning Middle Eastern politics.

Iran

Names/Greetings
Visitors to Iran should address their hosts by their last name or by their academic rank or title.

Appointments/Punctuality
Most business meetings are by appointment. Business sessions respect punctuality, whereas for social engagements it is not that important.

Iraq

Appointments/Punctuality
Prior appointments are necessary. However, do not be disturbed if your host fails to show up on time.

Hospitality/Gift Giving
You will discover that in Iraq — unlike other Arab countries — alcoholic beverages are available.

Conversation
It is advisable to avoid discussions of religion or Middle Eastern politics.

Jordan

General Protocol
The sales approach should not be high-pressured, and you probably will be subjected to group-style business meetings with friends and other businessmen.

Appointments/Punctuality
Prior appointments are a must, but do not be disappointed if your host is not punctual.

Conversation
Avoid any discussion of Middle Eastern politics.
Other subjects to avoid in conversation: religion, family, and the large amount of U.S. aid.

Lebanon

Appointments/Punctuality
Punctuality is not especially important.

Hospitality/Gift Giving
It is appropriate to talk about business only after the meal.
Flowers or candy are welcome gifts.
Gifts to be avoided include alcohol and cigarettes.

Conversation
The Lebanese appreciate compliments on such things as their homes, foods, and achievements.

Subjects suitable for conversation include business, children, education, and travel. Or tell funny stories.

Topics to avoid include politics, religion, and sex.

Saudi Arabia

General Protocol
Do not pull your hand away sharply if an Arab businessman, walking with you, takes your hand and holds it as you go. This is a nice sign of friendship, nothing more.

Names/Greetings
Customary greetings are elaborate. First, you say *salaam alaykum*; second, you shake hands while saying *kaif halak*; next, a Saudi may extend his left hand to your right shoulder and kiss you on both cheeks.

Appointments/Punctuality
Punctuality is desirable in Saudi Arabia.

Prior appointments are necessary, but you may find several other businesspeople present and several meetings occurring simultaneously.

Hospitality/Gift Giving
When invited to the home of an Arab businessman for dinner, skip your previous meal so that you have a keen appetite. Proper appreciation of a meal is shown by eating large quantities.

There are no nightclubs, no movie theatres, and very few restaurants.

Be careful about admiring your host's watch, cuff links, or other possessions. An Arab businessman is often very magnanimous. He might give them to you on the spot, and be offended if you refuse them.

Gifts are appreciated but not expected. Gifts to be avoided include liquor and items prohibited by Islam, such as photos and sculptures of women.

Conversation
Subjects to avoid in conversation include Middle Eastern politics and international oil politics.

**In the Arab countries, do not admire an object openly.
You may be the recipient of it.**

Syria

General Protocol
Do not be surprised if you arrive at a meeting to discover your host already occupied with someone else. It is common for Arabs to discuss business with several friends and other businessmen at once.

Appointments/Punctuality
Prior appointments are necessary, but do not be disturbed if your contact does not arrive on time.

Conversation
Subjects to avoid in conversation: Middle Eastern politics and international oil politics.

United Arab Emirates

General Protocol
The U.A.E. is a country, and is known as a country, that comprises the following sheikdoms: Abu Dhabi, Dubai, Sharjah, Ras al-Khaimah, Ajman, Umm al-Qaiwain, and Fujairah.

Most of the protocol and customs that apply in the other Middle Eastern, Moslem countries also apply in the U.A.E.

The U.A.E. are located on the Arabian Gulf— it is important to *not* refer to that body of water as the Persian Gulf. Other countries located on the Gulf in addition to the U.A.E. are Kuwait, Sultanate of Oman, Qatar, and Bahrain.

The Pacific and Asia

No region of the world has greater variety and diversity of languages, races, and religions than Asia, and the cultures of the countries of Asia and the Pacific have crisscrossed and inter-mingled for centuries.

General Protocol
Asians have an exquisite sense of politeness.

In most countries, but particularly in Southeast Asia, it is impolite to start talking business as soon as you sit down.

Although you might not receive clues from their outward appearance, you can be sure that your Asian counterpart is taking notice of yours— your behavior, your dress, the tailoring of your suit, the type of writing instrument you use.

Whatever happens, do not cause others to lose face. That's neither forgotten nor forgiven.

Appointments/Punctuality
Make appointments, keep them, and be punctual. However, do not be offended if others are late.

You'll be pleased to know that English is the language of commerce throughout Asia and the Pacific.

If you have a serious interest in developing business in this region, it is simply good business to read up on the country you are visiting and to know its culture and history.

You should arrange to have business cards printed in English and the local language. Businesspeople will find they will use many cards during their visit to each country.

Australia

General Protocol
Of all the countries of the region, Australia is probably the one in which Westerners, particularly Americans, feel the most comfortable. There is a great reservoir of warm feeling that has lasted since World War II.

Australians are direct, like Americans, and tell it like it is.

While the Australians tend to dress more casually than their British counterparts, they are just as big on form and procedure.

Names/Greetings
People like to be given a hearty handshake and called by their names.

Appointments/Punctuality
Punctuality is highly regarded. Prior appointments are necessary.

Hospitality/Gift Giving
It is acceptable to take flowers for the hostess or a bottle of wine when invited for lunch or dinner.

Bangladesh

Names/Greetings
When introduced to a man, it is customary to shake hands. When introduced to a woman, merely nod and speak a greeting.

Appointments/Punctuality
Punctuality is highly regarded.

Hospitality/Gift Giving
You may be entertained in a hotel or club. It is very unusual for wives to accompany their husbands to such functions.

Conversation
Avoid criticizing the country or the government.

The People's Republic of China

General Protocol
You should refer to their country as the "People's Republic of China" or simply "China."

The Chinese consider tipping anyone an insult, although exceptions are starting to appear.

Names/Greetings
A slight bow is appropriate when meeting someone. A handshake is also acceptable.

The Chinese are quite formal and will use the full title of their guests during introductions.

Appointments/Punctuality
Foreign businessmen usually find that their trip to China is highly organized and that punctuality is very important.

Prior appointments are necessary. Be prepared to wait a long time for Chinese businessmen to reach a decision.

Hospitality/Gift Giving
A visit to a Chinese home is rare — unless the government has given prior approval.

Guests should plan to arrive a little early and should leave shortly after the meal. During the meal, be prepared with toasts expressing thanks, pleasure, and friendship.

Gifts of any great value can cause embarrassment and usually are not accepted by the Chinese.

Conversation
Good topics for discussion include differences between China and the West, and the advances the Chinese have made.

Avoid mentioning Taiwan and do not criticize Chinese leadership.

Fiji

General Protocol
The custom is to remove your shoes when entering a house.

Names/Greetings
Fijians greet one another with a smile and raised eyebrows. Handshakes are appropriate.

Appointments/Punctuality
Punctuality is not important.

Hospitality/Gift Giving
Gifts are appreciated. It is customary to drink a cup of *kava* when visiting. Refusal to drink *kava* with the people is often taken as an insult.

Hong Kong

General Protocol
The people of Hong Kong are reserved and formal in almost all situations.

Avoid conflicts that would cause the Chinese to lose face.

Blue and white are the Chinese colors for mourning and should be avoided.

Names/Greetings
Handshakes are common when greeting and leaving.

Appointments/Punctuality
When appointments are made, a 30-minute "courtesy time" often is allotted. However, businessmen are usually punctual.

Hospitality/Gift Giving
A guest will take a gift of fruit, candy, or cookies when invited to dinner and will present it to the hostess with both hands.

Gifts are exchanged at the time of Chinese New Year (usually around February).

Conversation
The word for "thank you" is pronounced "doe-jay."

The political situation in China is controversial and political discussions should be avoided.

India

General Protocol
Hindus do not eat any beef. The cow is a sacred animal.

Muslims do not eat pork and strict Muslims do not drink alcohol.

Orthodox Sikhs wear a turban, and do not smoke, eat beef, or cut their hair.

Names/Greetings
Men may shake hands with other men when meeting or leaving. If introduced to a woman, a man should not shake hands but should place his palms together and bow slightly. Men should

avoid touching a woman and should not talk to a lone woman in public.

Appointments/Punctuality
Punctuality is advisable.

Hospitality/Gift Giving
While orthodox Muslim women are usually kept from the view of men, husbands should be invited to bring their wives to a social function.

Always use your right hand to accept or pass food.

Guests may take gifts such as fruit and candy or they may take gifts for the children in the family.

Conversation
Indians enjoy conversations on cultural achievements, Indian traditions, other people, and foreign countries.

Avoid discussions of personal affairs and India's poverty, military expenditures, and huge foreign aid.

Indonesia

General Protocol
Shoes should be removed before entering carpeted rooms and holy places — especially mosques.

Business dealings are usually long, slow, and frustrating.

Names/Greetings
Handshaking and a nod of the head are proper when you are introduced for the first time.

Appointments/Punctuality
Punctuality is important. Prior appointments are recommended.

Hospitality/Gift Giving
It is polite to take flowers when invited to dinner.

While visitors are not expected to eat only with the right hand, do not touch food with the left hand.

Indonesians generally do not expect gifts, but compliments and notes of appreciation are always welcome.

Conversation
Avoid the subjects of local politics, socialism, and foreign aid.

Japan

Names/Greetings
The usual form of greeting is a bow and not a handshake. Be prepared to exchange business cards.

Never surprise your Japanese host with a gift.
He may not be in a position to reciprocate immediately.

Never address a Japanese by his first name. Only his family and very close friends use the first name.

To say "Mister (last name)," simply say the last name and add the word *san*.

Appointments/Punctuality
Punctuality is advisable for both business and social engagements.

Hospitality/Gift Giving
Entertainment of visitors at private homes is not very frequent. When invited to a Japanese home, remove your hat and gloves once inside the entrance to the house and then remove your shoes. It is not customary to take flowers for the hostess, but take a box of cakes or candy.

If you are offered a gift, thank the person and wait for one or two more offers before accepting it. Receive the gift with both hands.

The Japanese enjoy receiving gifts, which should be wrapped in pastel-colored paper, no bows. They particularly relish gifts of brandy and frozen steaks. Gifts given in multiples of two are supposed to bring good luck, so such things as cuff links and pen and pencil sets are especially well-received.

Visitors should be prepared to be invited by their business colleagues to lavish dinner parties which may last for hours. These parties are almost always held in Japanese restaurants or nightclubs.

Conversation
One topic to be avoided: World War II.

Malaysia

General Protocol
Before entering a home, remove your shoes and sunglasses.

Names/Greetings
The handshake is common among men but rare between men and women — especially those of the older generation.

Appointments/Punctuality
Punctuality is expected. Prior appointments are advisable.

Hospitality/Gift Giving
Chinese eat with chopsticks and a spoon. Indians and Malays eat with their hands and a spoon. Hindus and some Buddhists do not eat beef. Muslims do not eat pork.

Entertainment is an important part of business arrangements and will probably be at a restaurant.

At Muslim dinners, never use the left hand to touch food. Follow the lead of the host to be sure.

It is not common to present gifts, but products from your company or the U.S. are most welcome.

Conversation
Subjects Malays like to talk about include politics, family, sports, and food.

New Zealand

Names/Greetings
Shake hands on meeting and leaving. Wait for women to offer their hands first.

Appointments/Punctuality
Prior appointments are advisable and visitors should try to be a bit early.

Hospitality/Gift Giving
Visitors usually invite customers to lunch at a hotel or restaurant. Otherwise, business meetings will be at the host's office. If you are invited to a New Zealander's home for a meal, you could take a modest gift of chocolates or whiskey.

Conversation
New Zealanders like to talk about national and international politics, the weather, and sports.

Topics to avoid include racial issues. Do not include New Zealand as part of "Australasia."

Pakistan

Names/Greetings
The common greeting is the handshake. Close friends may embrace. A man should not shake hands with a woman or touch her in public.

Use last name and title when addressing a Pakistani.

Appointments/Punctuality
Although Pakistanis are not time conscious, they will expect their Western visitors to arrive on time.

Most businesses are closed on Fridays.

Hospitality/Gift Giving
It is not unusual for a man to be invited to dinner without his wife. Even if the wife is invited to dinner, a man often will come alone.

Many of the traditional foods are eaten by hand and it is important to use only the right hand when eating.

While the Pakistanis are forbidden to eat pork, they enjoy beef, lamb, and poultry. The use of alcoholic beverages is not encouraged.

Conversation
It is advisable to avoid discussion of politics.

The Philippines

General Protocol
Americans usually feel at home in the Philippines. Americans are generally well-liked and the American life-style is emulated. English is the language of government, business, and education.

Names/Greetings
The everyday greeting for acquaintances is a handshake with men and women, and occasionally a pat on the back for men.

Appointments/Punctuality
Although time is flexible, it is advisable to be punctual.

Hospitality/Gift Giving
In a few homes, it is customary to remove one's shoes before entering the house. The guest should follow the example of the host.

If a gift is given — such as flowers — it is given on arrival. Thank-you notes are appreciated.

Conversation
Topics to avoid are politics, religion, local conditions, corruption, and foreign aid.

Filipinos are extremely family-oriented and conversation about their family is usually welcome. A note of caution: some Filipinos are strongly anti-American and this should be borne in mind.

Samoa

Names/Greetings
A formal greeting is usually given before a business meeting begins.

Hospitality/Gift Giving
It is customary to remove one's shoes before entering the house. Visitors should not enter a Samoan home until mats have been placed on the floor. They will sit cross-legged on the mats.

Even though fingers are used when eating in a Samoan home, in most cases visitors will be provided with utensils.

The *kava* ceremony is a sacred and highly respected custom in Samoa. If served *kava*, before you start drinking, hold the cup out in front of you and spill a few drops.

Singapore

General Protocol
Shoes are removed before one enters a mosque and sometimes before one enters a home.

Streets and other places are kept wonderfully clean due to harsh penalties against littering. So, be careful where you drop that cigarette butt.

Names/Greetings
Due to the influence of the British, Singapore is quite Westernized. However, the customs of the many ethnic groups are also followed, so greetings vary.

The handshake is the most common greeting— with a slight bow to the Orientals.

Appointments/Punctuality
Western visitors are expected to be punctual. Prior appointments are advisable.

Hospitality/Gift Giving
Entertainment usually takes the form of a lunch or dinner.

Do not use your left hand when eating with a Malay or an Indian.

Should you be invited to a Singapore home for dinner, a box of chocolates or flowers would be appreciated.

Conversation
Topics to avoid in conversation include religion and politics.

Subjects that are acceptable to discuss are travel experiences, news of countries visited, and economic advances of Singapore.

South Korea

General Protocol
Avoid talking or laughing loudly in any situation. Koreans, especially the women, cover their mouths when laughing.

Women's liberation has not been accepted yet. Men go through doors first. Women help men with their coats.

Blowing your nose in front of others is considered bad manners.

Names/Greetings
Men greet each other by bowing slightly and shaking hands with both hands or with the right hand. Women usually do not shake hands.

Family names come first, then the given name. It is difficult to distinguish male from female names in Korea.

Appointments/Punctuality
Prior appointments are necessary and, while punctuality is not of great importance, Westerners are usually expected to arrive on time.

Hospitality/Gift Giving
Shoes are always removed before entering a Korean home or Korean restaurant.

Business entertainment is considered very important and is usually limited to restaurants and bars. Wives are rarely included.

All courses of a meal are served at once.

If you are invited to a Korean home, it would be appropriate to take flowers or a small gift, to be offered with both hands. Gifts are not opened in front of the giver.

Conversation
Avoid discussions of socialism, communism, internal politics, and criticism of the government.

Sri Lanka

Names/Greetings
Because of the strong influence of the British, English greetings are suitable.

Appointments/Punctuality
It is considered polite to respect punctuality. Prior appointments are necessary.

Hospitality/Gift Giving
Sri Lankans are hospitable and courteous. It is the usual custom for them to offer visitors tea at the beginning of a meeting. Tea is the national drink.

Tahiti

Names/Greetings
Most people shake hands when they meet. Tahitians usually kiss each other on the cheeks when greeting.

Hospitality/Gift Giving
If invited to a Tahitian's home, you should express interest in your host's home and family. But be careful— your Tahitian host might make a gift of a prized possession if you express too great an interest in it.

Tahitians remove their shoes when entering a home.

Tahitian food is eaten with the fingers.

Taiwan

General Protocol
Taiwanese businessmen can take a long time by American standards to reach a decision, so be patient.

Names/Greetings
A handshake is customary when meeting acquaintances and close friends. A nod of the head is appropriate when meeting someone for the first time.

Appointments/Punctuality
If you arrive at your appointment shortly before or after the scheduled time, that is perfectly acceptable.

Hospitality/Gift Giving
Entertainment is usually offered in restaurants and not in the home.

Taiwanese meals are elaborate and exhausting. Be prepared to eat sparingly during the early stages of what could be a 20-course meal. Toasts are common; *kampai* means "bottoms up."

Chopsticks and a ceramic spoon are the common eating utensils in Taiwan.

A small gift, such as fruit, candy, or cookies, is appropriate when visiting a family at home. Both hands should be used when handing a gift or other object to another person.

Shoes are not worn in some homes. Observe the host.

Thank-you notes are a must and are appreciated.

Conversation
Avoid discussing mainland China and local politics.

Thailand

General Protocol
Avoid stepping on doorsills, where Thai tradition says a spirit resides.

Never point to anything casually with your foot. When standing or seated, never angle your foot in such a way that it is conspicuous or that the sole is visible.

Never touch a person's head — even a child's — as the head is considered the seat of the soul.

Thai businessmen take a long time to reach a decision. Be patient.

Names/Greetings
Thais do not usually shake hands except in more westernized social groups. The traditional and most common Thai greeting — the *wai* — is made by placing both hands together in a prayer position at the chest.

Don't be surprised if you are addressed by your first name — for instance, "Mr. Bob" or "Miss Mary" — instead of your surname.

Appointments/Punctuality
Prior appointments are necessary and punctuality is a sign of courtesy.

Hospitality/Gift Giving
It is customary to remove your shoes when entering a Thai home.

Normally, small souvenirs make acceptable gifts. Gifts usually should be wrapped. Flowers make suitable gifts.

Conversation
Topics to avoid in conversation include politics, the Royal Family, and religion.

Tonga

Names/Greetings
Handshaking and a spoken greeting are customary.

Tongans usually call people by their first name.

Hospitality/Gift Giving
Gifts are appropriate but are expected only from close friends. Flowers are not regarded as gifts.

While utensils are often used at the table, Tongans prefer to eat with their hands.

Central and South America

It is important to recognize diversity in Latin America. Customs, phrases, and behavior may not be the same in Argentina as in Colombia. There are some fairly safe generalizations, though, and here are some of them.

General Protocol

Latin Americans tend to stand close during conversation. If you want to do business in this part of the world, learn to accept your host's distance.

The main meal of the day is at noon throughout Latin America.

Tipping varies according to country.

Names/Greetings

In much of Central and South America, the custom is to shake hands both on arrival and departure.

Arrange to have business cards printed in English and the local language.

Appointments/Punctuality

As for punctuality, a 30-minute delay is customary.

Hospitality/Gift Giving

Latin Americans are warm and friendly people. They enjoy entertaining.

It is customary to give gifts. Appropriate gifts for ladies include perfume and name brand items; for men, novelties or men's accessories, also name brands; for both, unique items with an art/history relationship from your homeland.

When you are invited to a home for dinner, flowers or good wine and liquors make suitable gifts. Toasts are common, but let the host say his first, then be prepared with your own.

Dress

Wear proper attire (jacket and tie) even if the climate is warmer than that to which you are accustomed.

Conversation

Topics for conversation could include mention of local folklore customs, historic dates, or heroes.

Argentina

Names/Greetings

Men, when meeting after a long absence, hug each other (*abrazo*). Women will shake hands with both hands and kiss each other on the cheek.

Appointments/Punctuality

Prior appointments are necessary.

Don't go native.

Hospitality/Gift Giving
Gifts to be avoided include personal items such as ties and shirts.

If a visitor is entertained in an Argentine home, he should arrange to send flowers or candy to his hostess.

Conversation
Argentines welcome compliments about their children, the meal, and their home.

Avoid discussion of controversial subjects such as politics and religion.

Feel free to talk about sports — particularly soccer — and the beauty of the local parks and gardens.

Bolivia

General Protocol
Your attempts to use Spanish will be appreciated.

Names/Greetings
Handshakes are common. Bolivians often greet friends and acquaintances with a spoken salutation.

Appointments/Punctuality
Visitors should be punctual, even if others are late.

Hospitality/Gift Giving
Bolivians expect visitors to eat everything on their plate. Therefore, you should take a small portion of each type of food offered.

Flowers and small gifts are usually given to the host. Gifts are customarily opened after the giver has left.

Entertainment for businessmen is normally a luncheon or dinner in a restaurant. Wives do not normally attend such events.

Conversation
Generally, any subject can be discussed, although it would be well to avoid politics and religion.

Brazil

General Protocol
Remember, Portuguese is the language of Brazil.

Names/Greetings
Brazilians feel no shame in showing their emotions and will embrace on the street. Men and women always shake hands upon meeting and leaving. When women meet, they exchange kisses by placing their cheeks together and kissing the air.

Appointments/Punctuality
Brazilians, like most Latin Americans, are casual about both time and work. Never start right into business discussions unless your host does so first.

Hospitality/Gift Giving
Expect to be frequently served small cups of very strong coffee.

If a visitor has been entertained in a home, it is polite to send flowers to the hostess the next day with a thank-you note. Be sure the flowers are not purple (a sign of death).

Conversation
Brazilians are very proud of their children and appreciate your attention to them. Brazilian men love good jokes and love to laugh, but avoid ethnic jokes and do not discuss Argentina.

Chile

Names/Greetings
When people are first introduced, a handshake is customary as is a kiss on the right cheek. Male Chileans may greet one another with hearty *abrazos* (hugs), with women customarily kissing each other on the cheek.

Appointments/Punctuality
Prior appointments are necessary and Chilean businessmen respect punctuality.

Hospitality/Gift Giving
Business entertaining generally is done at major hotels and restaurants.

When visiting a home, guests should wait outside the door until invited inside.

A gift of a bouquet of flowers to the hostess is appropriate.

Conversation
Topics to be avoided in conversation include local politics and religion.

Chileans are pleased if guests show an interest in their family and especially in their children.

Colombia

General Protocol
Colombian businessmen prefer slow deliberations and like quiet discussions over black Colombian coffee before any business is transacted.

Be sure to plan to relax the first day in Bogotá — the altitude may affect you.

Names/Greetings
A handshake is the customary greeting. Men will shake hands with everyone when entering a home or group and also when leaving. Women do not usually shake hands with other women; they clasp forearms.

Hospitality/Gift Giving
When a visitor is invited to a home, it is customary to send a gift of fruit, flowers, or chocolates before arrival, if time permits. If not, send a gift afterwards, with a thank-you note.

Gifts should not be personal unless you know the person very well. Then you may give a tie to a man and perfume to a woman.

Conversation
The Colombians will appreciate your interest in sports — particularly soccer — art, Colombian coffee, and the beauty of the countryside. Bullfighting is popular in Colombia and Colombians would resent any adverse comments from visitors.

Costa Rica

Names/Greetings
When greeting, men always shake hands; women who are friends or relatives kiss each other once on the cheek.

Hospitality/Gift Giving
People frequently exchange gifts of all kinds on special occasions.

Ecuador

General Protocol
Relax on your first day in Ecuador. You may have trouble breathing until you become accustomed to the high altitude.

Most stores close at siesta time, which lasts about two hours.

Names/Greetings
The handshake is used when meeting someone for the first time. Women who are close friends kiss each other, and men embrace.

Hospitality/Gift Giving
A visitor compliments new things in the home. After a meal in the home, each visitor should thank the host or hostess profusely.

Conversation
It is advisable to avoid political topics and any issues that imply the superiority of the U.S.

El Salvador

General Protocol
It is not polite for someone from the U.S. to introduce himself as an "American." Salvadorans are also American.

Names/Greetings
Handshaking is the usual form of greeting, although some people merely nod when meeting.

Hospitality/Gift Giving
A guest should compliment the person who has prepared the food — and especially compliment the hostess.

Guatemala

General Protocol
It is advisable to discuss business affairs outside the home and away from the family.

Names/Greetings
It is appropriate to shake hands when meeting someone and to say something in Spanish, if possible. Men greet each other with a handshake, and close friends embrace and pat each other on the back. Close women friends usually give a gentle hug and a kiss on the cheek.

Hospitality/Gift Giving
Dinner guests may take small gifts such as flowers or candy.

Honduras

General Protocol
Machismo — the idea that men are superior to women — prevails.

Names/Greetings
Close acquaintances often greet each other with a hearty hug *(abrazo).* Otherwise, a handshake is sufficient. Women who know each other often exchange a kiss on the cheek.

Mexico

General Protocol
Mexico City's high altitude, smog, and wild traffic should be respected and anticipated — and, to compound the problem, unless care is taken about drinking water, the visitor may suffer diarrhea, commonly called "Montezuma's Revenge." All this is

negated, however, by a friendly, gracious, and easygoing business atmosphere.

Mexicans appreciate a visitor's effort to speak Spanish.

Names/Greetings
Handshakes are customary. However, longtime friends may engage in a full embrace — the *abrazo*. Women often greet each other with a kiss on the cheek.

Hospitality/Gift Giving
While it is not customary to take gifts, they are appreciated. Gifts may be wrapped and presented as you would in the U.S.

Flowers are not expected by host or hostess and thank-you notes are not common but are appreciated. If you do send flowers, remember that yellow flowers connote death, red flowers cast spells, and white ones lift the spells.

Conversation
Avoid political and historical topics — such as the Mexican-American War and illegal aliens — in conversation.

Safe topics of conversation include the weather, fashion, and travel.

Nicaragua

General Protocol
Machismo — the concept that men are superior to women — prevails.

Names/Greetings
When meeting someone, it is appropriate to smile, shake hands, and say a greeting (in Spanish, if possible). Men greet each other with a handshake. Close friends embrace and pat each other on the back. Women usually give a gentle hug and kiss each other on the cheek.

Hospitality/Gift Giving
Dinner guests may take small gifts, such as flowers or candy.

Panama

General Protocol
Americans who do not mingle with the local people are considered cold and aloof.

Machismo, the concept that men are superior to women, prevails.

Names/Greetings
Friends nod and embrace when they meet. A handshake is appropriate among business associates.

Hospitality/Gift Giving
Food or seedlings are appropriate as gifts when visiting the interior of Panama.

Conversation
In conversation, avoid discussion of local politics and the former Canal Zone.

Paraguay

Names/Greetings
When people first meet, the greeting *mucho gusto* is often used. People stand very close when conversing and men often embrace on meeting. Women usually kiss each other on both cheeks. Close friends may walk arm in arm.

Hospitality/Gift Giving
When visiting a home, the guest usually greets the host with a short, formal speech and asks permission to enter.

Conversation
Topics suitable for conversation include the family, sports, current events, and the weather. Paraguayans are very proud of their hydroelectric dams.

It is not advisable to discuss politics.

Peru

General Protocol
The Peruvians are conservative, formal, and proud of their Inca and Spanish colonial backgrounds.

Names/Greetings
Men and women shake hands when meeting and parting. Men often greet close friends with a hug. Close women friends often greet each other with a kiss on the cheek.

Hospitality/Gift Giving
Gifts of flowers are appropriate for any occasion.

Most dinner invitations are for 9 P.M. — or later. It is considered correct to arrive a half hour after the stated time for dinner. The only event that requires absolute punctuality is a bullfight.

Conversation
In conversation, all topics except local politics are acceptable.

Uruguay

Names/Greetings
Handshaking is the usual way of greeting.

Hospitality/Gift Giving
While most entertaining is done in restaurants, a visitor may be invited to an Uruguayan's home. Remember to send flowers or chocolates to your hostess before the occasion.

Conversation
In conversation, avoid the subject of politics. Communism is a very sensitive subject and should not be mentioned.

Uruguayans like to talk about sports — especially soccer.

Venezuela

Names/Greetings
Men greet each other with a hug and women greet each other with an embrace and a kiss on the cheek. Handshaking is also common.

Appointments/Punctuality
The average Venezuelan businessman is very busy and you should be prepared to be direct and to the point in discussions.

Hospitality/Gift Giving
Venezuelans usually invite only special close friends to their homes. Flowers sent to the host or hostess before an event will be appreciated. Otherwise, take flowers or candy when you arrive — or send a thank-you note after the event.

An appropriate gift for a man is something for the office — such as a good-quality pen. A woman would appreciate the gift of an orchid — the national flower.

The Caribbean

The Caribbean area comprises independent countries as well as territories which presently are or formerly were closely associated with Great Britain, France, Holland, and the United States. There is a wide variety of races, languages, and cultures. A visitor to the Caribbean area may want to keep in mind the following general tips.

General Protocol
While English is the prevailing language, other languages include Spanish, French, Dutch, and several dialects.

Names/Greetings
Generally, people shake hands when meeting and parting.

Visitors should be prepared to have a supply of business cards printed in English and the local language (if other than English).

Appointments/Punctuality
Prior appointments are advisable. Punctuality is not closely adhered to in the region.

Hospitality/Gift Giving
Table manners are very informal.

Dress
Casual warm-weather clothing is acceptable in most areas.

Conversation
While it is acceptable to discuss the economy, the tourist business, and the weather, it is advisable to avoid discussing local politics, religion, and controversial subjects, particularly race.

Haiti

General Protocol
French is spoken in Haiti.

At 8 A.M. and at 6 P.M., a bugle is played and a flag raised. If in the vicinity— either on foot or in a car— you are expected to stop, get out of the car, and stand respectfully.

Hospitality/Gift Giving
It is not necessary to take a gift on the first trip, but a gift should be taken on the second visit. The gift may be of modest value — something unusual from the U.S. would be appreciated.

Conversation
Avoid political discussions. The rare beauty of Haitian native art is a safe and easy topic.

Puerto Rico

General Protocol
Visitors who attempt to speak some Spanish are appreciated, but almost all Puerto Ricans speak English.

Names/Greetings
People shake hands when they meet. Close friends often embrace. Women may grasp each other's shoulders and kiss on the cheek. People stand very close when talking.

Hospitality/Gift Giving
Gifts are given freely and they are unwrapped immediately when received.

Conversation
Puerto Ricans object to open criticism, "pushiness," and greed.

Puerto Ricans appreciate discussing their cultural heritage and their rapid economic growth. But statehood with the U.S. is a hotly debated and divisive issue.

North America

Canada

Canada maintains strong links with Great Britain, other European countries, and its neighbor to the south, the United States. A large part of the population is French-speaking. In spite of their differences, both French-speaking and English-speaking Canadians live together as one nation.

General Protocol
Canadians are somewhat more conservative than U.S. citizens.

Names/Greetings
Shaking hands at meeting and parting is appropriate.

Appointments/Punctuality
Punctuality is expected in most of Canada.

Hospitality/Gift Giving
Most entertaining is done in restaurants and clubs.

If you are entertained in a private home, it would be courteous to take or send flowers to your hostess. Avoid sending white lilies; they are associated with funerals.

Conversation
In conversation, avoid taking sides on partition — separation into separate states, French and Canadian.

Canadians are proud of their country and take exception to exaggerated comparisons with the U.S.

Mentioning positive examples and making favorable comments about the people and their country are most welcome.

CHAPTER 3

Gift Giving
and
Receiving

Gift Giving Gaffes
or
Doing it wrong can be worse than not doing it at all

On other continents, in other cultures, giving and getting are no idle pastimes. Whether you offer a five-course dinner at the Ritz or a 50¢ company calendar, it is an occasion that calls for knowing the rules and how they got that way. Sensitivities on the subject vary wildly from country to country, bubbling up out of the national psyche of history, geography, social and religious pressures, and local prides and prejudices. The ill-considered gift can easily turn out to be comparable to an exploding cigar.

Why does handing your hostess in Brussels a cheery bouquet of chrysanthemums cast a pall over the party? What makes your Chinese client recoil when you give him a shiny new desk clock? (In these different cultures, the answer is the same: each happens to be a reminder of death.)

Nor is the touchiness all on the side of the givee. "Blush and thrust" is how one U.S. executive describes the technique employed by many American businessmen unused to the exchange of gifts and entertainment with virtual strangers.

Hoping to eliminate the blush and thrust, as well as to simplify a many-sided subject, Dr. Kathleen Reardon, a professor of communication sciences and specialist in persuasion theory, conducted research sponsored by The Parker Pen Company among some 125 of America's best-traveled executives. The findings of the Reardon research (pages 119 to 135) reveal how important this international exchange process has become and how to practice it smoothly.

The Mighty Pen

At this point, we would be disloyal indeed if we did not mention why pens make the perfect gift.

- Everyone writes. You don't know if everyone smokes (so a lighter may be inappropriate), or if they use cuff links, or if their religion permits them to drink alchohol, or if their wife will like the brightly colored scarf you have selected. But pens are safe, safe, safe.

- Pens are portable. You can easily pack a goodly number in your suitcase. Moreover, you can take along an assortment — some modestly priced, others with a bit more luxury— to fit different circumstances.

103

**In the People's Republic of China, never give the gift of a clock.
A clock is a symbol of bad luck.**

- They are used — daily. After all, the purpose of any gift is usefulness, and, if at all possible, frequent use. A pen is used more than any other personal accessory and is, therefore, a constant reminder of the giver.

Over 80 percent of Parker Pen's sales come from outside the U.S., so their pens are known and respected throughout the world. And obtaining repair service and refills is not a problem, because pens are sold in literally every country in the world.

The founder, George S. Parker, sold his first pen overseas in 1902. He was fond of saying, "Our pens not only make perfect gifts, but they will write in every language as well."

Now, let's move on to an examination of the whole realm of do's and don'ts in the important areas of gift giving and entertaining. Both are just as important in communicating goodwill as are proper protocol, body language, and gestures.

Money talks — often much too loudly

"It's the thought that counts" really does count — often, more than cost. That is not to say that the next time you get a Rolex you should return the favor with a box of candy. But no matter how much you spend, take the trouble to think of the recipient not as a company or a client but as a person — someone, for example, who has always dreamed of visiting the American West someday. In which case, a shimmering Ansel Adams print of Yosemite can say more about your goodwill than a gold ingot.

"No business problem gets solved by simply throwing money at it — and that includes what to give the client," says a corporate spokeswoman in the sporting goods business. A gesture too lavish can cause more embarrassment than one too modest. It may smack of *baksheesh, dash* — or whatever the local payola is called. Or it may burden the recipient with an unwanted obligation, a particularly serious blunder in Asian cultures where duty is taken very seriously.

Footloose and tariff-free

The U.S. citizen entering a foreign country where import duties are prohibitive has a big advantage in playing Santa, not only to foreign hosts but to Americans in his own firm working over there. In many places, tariffs on luxury goods raise the price of a bottle of Scotch by $50, whereas you can get it for $10 in the airport tax-free shop. This is also true of sporting goods, jewelry, pens, lighters, cigarettes, etc. So even though the gift may be costing you peanuts, the person to whom you give it will be very grateful.

Dropping certain famous American brand names usually has a magical effect on the natives, whether they are Parisians or Masai. Bloomingdale's, Tiffany, Levi's, Steuben. Even L.L. Bean is becoming a household word where no lumberjacket or pup tent had dared cross the border until recently. Again, it is the thought (or in this case the label) that counts, not the price tag.

If you are still at a loss to know what to give, bring something for the children. Almost anything American, from yo-yos to magic markers and Muppet dolls to Disneyland T-shirts, gets a warm reception. For businesswomen who anticipate having to reciprocate, it is polite to give the men you work with overseas house gifts rather than personal gifts — an American cookbook if you know the wife is fluent in English; a subscription to an American magazine if you know the home address; typical bits of Americana such as patchwork pillow covers, beeswax candles, Indian pottery, Vermont maple syrup, or a Cheddar cheese.

It is usually better to shop here for giving there. In foreign lands, even the most prosaic American goods seem exotic — especially to wives and children, who in many parts of the world never get to leave the homeland, much less shop at Macy's.

In Japan, the way a gift is wrapped is at least as important as what is inside. If you take your Oriental hosts something from home, make sure it is not the sort of thing they specialize in themselves. The twentieth century version of coals to Newcastle is pocket calculators to Kyoto.

Whatever you give, avoid waiting until you get home and then sending it. The recipient is likely to suffer more inconvenience and expense at Customs than your largesse can ever justify.

On the receiving end

When it is time to say thank you, do not let the sound of your own voice carry the message. Make it memorable and write. But if you put off all your bread-and-butter notes until you are back at the office, they will probably never get written. One piece of advice from experienced travelers: take personalized stationery with you and mail your thank-yous as you go along. This way, you can always check the spelling of names, confirm addresses, save on intercontinental airmail — *and* get word to all you have met before the memory is out of mind (yours and theirs).

And if you happen to have taken pictures along the way that included your host (at his home, on a sightseeing tour, even at his pig-iron plant), enclosing prints of the most flattering shots will almost certainly get you another invitation to the blast furnaces anytime you want to go.

Dinner at nine, ten, or when?

The head of a company's Mexico City office was required to entertain often and thought he knew Latin ways. So when a local dignitary invited him to bring the firm's top management from New York to dinner at his palatial Mexico City penthouse, the American exec had them all there promptly at nine.

Only the maid, however, was at home — with not a knife, fork, or host in sight. By ten o'clock, the president began to look darkly at his local exec. By eleven, so did the chairman of the board. Five minutes later, the host breezed in — in golf clothes. What was everyone doing there so early, he wanted to know. Of course, the invitation said nine, but in Mexico City's social circles, who shows up on time? By midnight, the host was properly dressed and dinner was finally served.

Whether you are host or guest, it is useful to know local attitudes toward punctuality. Both time and space can be very subjective concepts, depending on where you are.

One of the reasons, for instance, for being fashionably late in Mexico City is that it boasts the worst traffic jams in the entire world. In fact, the only time of day when anyone is expected to be even remotely on time is for early-morning breakfast meetings, before traffic paralysis sets in. Hence, you should seek advice on not just when to arrive (or to expect others to) but also how long it is likely to take to get there.

Among those least tolerant of lateness — particularly for business meetings, but only slightly less for social situations — the Japanese, Germans, Scandinavians, and British head the list. In the Middle East, they expect you to be punctual but then keep things going hours longer than you might anticipate. There is no such thing as a mini-meeting or a quick lunch with an Arab. Therefore, try not to schedule either business or social events back to back.

Tipping

Has a traveler ever encountered anyone who didn't expect a tip? Columbus probably disembarked with plenty of small change in his pocket.

There are places where tipping is an insult, of course, but they are few — primarily China, Iceland, and Tahiti — and far between. Elsewhere, it pays to know how much or how little you have to pay.

No matter what the guidebooks say (including this one) if you are visiting a country for the first time, always ask at your hotel or among your business contacts there what the local tipping rules are. Times and customs are quick to change, especially where large numbers of Western visitors are a new experience for the locals. What was an insult yesterday may have become a way of life by today.

Nearly everywhere outside the U.S., it is customary for hotel and restaurant bills to include a service charge of between ten percent and twenty percent (higher in some South American countries). If you do not see it marked on menu or check, ask the maitre d' if it is included or not. When it is, the usual practice is to add another five percent to restaurant bills. Where service is not included, doormen, porters, and chambermaids also expect something extra, though less than you would pay here.

Rules for tipping taxi drivers vary with the country — and sometimes with the driver. In most of the Middle East, for example, drivers theoretically do not get tipped. But once you are in the backseat you may find that the agreed-upon fare has suddenly doubled, in effect giving your driver a very nice gratuity: 100 percent.

Countries where there really is no taxi tip include Denmark, Holland, Finland, Switzerland, China, Japan, Singapore, Taiwan, Thailand, and most of Latin America excepting Argentina, Brazil, and Mexico.

Overtipping is offensive anywhere ("The capitalists are coming!"), but most of all in poor countries. In India, one *rupee* and change is always enough. Undertipping is in equally bad taste and is easy to do if you are unfamiliar with the currency. Giving a Thai a *baht*, for example, is like tossing a dime to the doorman at the Plaza Hotel. If you do not know what you are giving, then it's better to give nothing.

There may also be occasions when you will want to tip but not with cash. Tour guides, drivers, interpreters, stenographers, and others whose help is more personalized — or who are more highly qualified — than those who open doors, carry bags, and pour wine are often offended by an impersonal tip. If you expect to use any of these services, you will find it handy to take appropriate gifts with you. Again, something from the U.S. is usually more appreciated than a quick purchase in your hotel gift shop.

When is a tip a bribe? And vice versa?

That question has puzzled travelers for centuries, so if you're ever confronted with an outright bribe, you might as well know the terminology.

Baksheesh (bak-SHEESH) In Turkey, Egypt, India, and other Eastern countries, a gratuity or gift of alms.

Mordida (mor-DEE-da) Spanish for bribe. Especially known in Mexico. Literally, "a little bite."

Jeito (jay-EE-toe) Commonly used in Brazil. Signifies "you do me a favor, and I'll do you a favor." Can also mean "influence" in the sense of using influence to help. Does not usually involve an actual transfer of money.

Dash (dash) Used in various parts of Africa. A small monetary gift that is expected when getting anything from a visa to an airplane seat.

Grease (greese) Also, "facilitating payments." Refers to legal and permitted payments of modest sums to foreign officials for speedy action of their normal duties. Used almost everywhere, including the U.S.

Kumshaw (KUM-shaw) Southeast Asian term for bribe.

To Give a Gift:
How, When, What, Where

To our knowledge, no extensive research has ever been conducted — until now — on the subject of international gift giving. Moreover, those surveyed in a 1981 Parker Pen-sponsored study (see pages 119 to 121 for explanatory notes on research) added commendations and encouragement to do more. The head of protocol for a major government department affirmed that never before had she found this type of comprehensive information to be available.

So here we go around the world bearing gifts.

Gift Giving in Western Europe

1. It is usually considered crass to give a business gift at first encounter.

2. Flowers are customary for a dinner hostess, but it's better to send them ahead than to hand her the task of arranging them just when you arrive. It also avoids embarrassment for other arrivals who come empty-handed.

3. Avoid giving thirteen or any even number of flowers. It is bad luck.

4. To French-speaking people, chrysanthemums are associated with mourning. To French and Germans, red roses are a gift only between lovers.

5. Good chocolates and liqueurs are appropriate house gifts.

6. If the occasion calls for something more elaborate, small porcelain and silver gifts (table lighters, ashtrays, candlesticks, etc.) are always welcome.

7. Other home furnishings run the risk of clashing with their surroundings — and acting as a lasting reminder of a bad choice.

8. House gifts should always be given as soon as you arrive, not after dinner, thus implying payment for a good meal.

9. Perfume and men's cologne are usually too personal for a business gift to or from either sex.

10. Avoid logo gifts with large and prominent stamps of your company name.

11. Never give anything either cheap *or* extravagant, and that goes for wrappings as well.

12. Do not enclose your business card. Always use a blank card with a handwritten note.

13. In Germany, wrapping is very important, but do not use white, black, or brown gift paper or ribbon. Flowers should be presented *un*wrapped.

14. In France, gifts that appeal to intellect or aesthetics are especially appreciated — records, art prints, and, most of all, books, with the emphasis on the latest biographies, histories, criticisms, and memoirs of presidents and statesmen. (It is often months or years before American best-sellers are available over there in French or English, so do your shopping here.)

15. In Britain, entertainment in the form of lunch, dinner, drinks, or a night at the theater or ballet usually takes the place of gift giving.

Gift Giving in Japan

The Japanese give gifts under every conceivable circumstance — and some inconceivable ones. This rampant giftomania is explained by writer Shintaro Ryo as "goodwill forced on the recipients" largely for the purpose of creating "a vague sense of duty . . . and obligation."

The dark and disapproving headlines of past scandals, although they may have reduced the monetary value, have not reduced the trend. In fact, perfunctory, even valueless, gifts are the norm and have given birth to a practice called *tara imawashi*, whereby when you get a gift you have no use for you pass it on as a gift to meet your obligation to someone else.

There are four basic kinds of gift giving:

- *giri* (duty) giving as described above

- collective giving, which is *giri* giving but by a company or delegation of company representatives, thereby relieving the individual of obligation and keeping the transaction impersonal

- ulterior-motive giving, which by any other name could only be called a bribe

- personal giving when there is a genuine emotional bond

Whatever category you fall into, however, there are general rules of good manners and good taste.

1. There are two times when business gifts are obligatory: July 15 (the midyear of *Chugen*) and January 1 (year end or *Toshidama*).

2. Business gifts are frequently given at first meetings. But do not embarrass your Japanese counterpart by being the only one to show up with a gift.

3. In any situation, it is better to allow the other person to initiate the giving. After all, it is more *his* custom than *yours*, so why not give him the satisfaction of making the first move?

4. Also, avoid outgiving the Japanese — and, by implication, placing an obligation on them.

5. On the other hand, your return gift should not be dramatically inferior in value.

6. Unless you have something for everyone present, give your gift while the recipient is alone.

7. Do not expect him to open it in front of you, nor should you open yours unless he asks you to.

8. If he does open it, do not expect an effusive reaction, and you should be similarly restrained in yours.

9. Do not be insulted by perfunctory, more or less valueless, gifts. To a Japanese, it is more the ceremony than the sentiment that counts.

10. The same rule, however, does not apply to you. Never give tacky or jokey logo items such as imprinted matchbooks, T-shirts, caps, bumper stickers, cheap ballpoints, etc.

11. Also, do not give anything with the company name printed tastelessly large.

12. You will rarely if ever be invited to a Japanese home, but if you are, flowers are appropriate. Be sure to check with the florist that you are not arriving with the sixteen-petal chrysanthemums reserved for the Imperial Family crest.

13. Other welcome gifts include imported Scotch, cognac, and frozen steaks bought at tax-free airport shops.

14. The latest electronic toys are always popular with Japanese children — and their doting parents.

15. Gucci, Hermés, Countess Mara, Georg Jensen, and other tony brand names are a language virtually every Japanese understands.

16. If you give gold make sure it is heavy in karats. The Japanese prefer white precious metals.

17. Because of their predilection for opening their presents privately, never give the Japanese an unwrapped object, even if it is your company pen or desk calendar.

18. Perfunctory wrapping, however, is almost worse than none at all. If you do not have the knack (or the materials), either wait and buy your gifts at a Japanese department store or arrange

for someone who knows how it is done to wrap what you have brought.

19. If you do wrap the gift yourself, never use ribbons or bows bought in your country. The color and texture signify the type and value of the gift. Also, avoid boldly colored paper.

20. Black and white wrappings convey funereal overtones.

21. Bright red is also considered inappropriate for wrappings.

22. To show the best possible taste (and regard for the recipient), buy lightly tinted rice paper to do your wrapping when you get there.

23. When entertaining, you may not be able to match the lavish geisha-house treatment provided by your host, but do not cut corners with a quick round of sake or lunch at a noodle house.

24. Avoid gifts in multiples of fours. The number four has morbid connotations.

Gift Giving in the Arab World

Let your motto be, tread tactfully and carry a big gift. In a land with vast amounts of wealth, American visitors are often amazed to find generosity to match. Arabs both *give* big and expect to *get* big. Not out of venality, heaven knows. (The average per capita income in Saudi Arabia is over $50,000 a year, and just about any businessman you deal with could afford to cover both arms three-deep in Piagets.) Arabs are unusually sensitive to public shame and personal slights. Reciprocity is a matter of respectability, and no successful relationship can be one-way.

The Arab will always strive to outdo you in generosity. But he may keep tabs on how you do, too. And that goes not just for dollars and cents but for understanding his culture and respecting its achievements.

1. Never give liquor as a gift or ask for it to be served. It is forbidden by the Islamic religion.

2. Never give gifts for a wife or wives.

3. Gifts for children, however, are enthusiastically welcomed.

4. Do not give a gift at first meeting. It may be interpreted as a bribe.

5. Avoid junk gifts.

6. Gifts of intellectual value such as art, books, and records and tapes are advisable. So is office equipment, from desk sets to pocket calculators.

7. American and German workmanship is appreciated.

8. Do not appear to contrive to present the gift when the recipient is alone. Unless he is a personal friend, it will make you both look suspect.

9. Items depicting animals often have connotations of bad luck.

10. A company gift should never be impersonal but should reflect either the recipient's tastes or something special about the source. You might, say, have a paperweight made from the marble or stone of the firm's home state. Or an ornamental bowl engraved with the state flower.

11. Do not profusely admire any Arab's possessions or he may make a gift of them.

12. There is one exception to #11, however. To ask for an English-language copy of the teachings of Muhammad, called the *Koran* or *Quran*, is often flattering to your host — and useful in learning to understand him.

Gift Giving in Latin America

Enchufado is what Latins admiringly call a man who makes things happen — not with brains or brawn necessarily, but with his connectedness. In Mexico he is called a *coyote*, in Brazil, a *despechante*, but whatever the name, in the land of the insider, the outsider can only make things happen with the help of this "facilitator."

These examples of being on the inside demonstrate how important it is to meet a Latin on his terms. And his terms are very simple: he wants your friendship and he wants it now. No holds barred, literally. To a Northerner, this instant intimacy sometimes feels like assault and battery by *abrazo*. Another important aspect of the relationship is lavish giving and taking. Whether it is of money, favors, or gifts, it is a way of life outsiders find it hard not to get into. The trick is to do it with grace and genuine regard for your new "old friends."

Business gifts in Latin America should not be excessive.

To help with that aspect, here are general gift-giving guidelines for Latin America.

1. Never go empty-handed to anyone's home.

2. Do not come bearing business gifts until a friendly relationship has begun.

3. Women should be very cautious about giving gifts to male colleagues or customers. Even a business gift as dispassionate as a paperweight can look like a personal overture.

4. It is always appreciated when men or women give gifts for the children.

5. Do not give gifts during business. The best time is after business negotiations have been completed and in a relaxed social situation. The Latins' long, leisurely lunch provides an apt setting.

6. No matter what your relationship with the recipient, your first consideration should be whether the gift is appropriate to his needs and taste, not how much it costs.

7. For your return visit, it is thoughtful to ask your Latin colleagues if there is anything from America they especially want. Small appliances are popular, but unless you are asked to bring them, the implication can be that U.S.-made goods are better than anything Latin American.

8. Logo gifts should offer a unique connection with your company and not just be a vehicle for its name. For instance, a lighter made from material your firm manufactures or a symbol of the part of the country where your headquarters are (marble from Georgia, say).

9. Giving perfume to women is not considered too personal a gift.

10. Avoid giving the following: thirteen of anything (bad luck), anything black or purple (a reminder of the somber Lenten season), knives (imply cutting off a relationship), and handkerchiefs (associated with tears).

11. Do not admire a Latin's possessions effusively or he is very likely to insist on making a gift of them. One businessman was forced to accept a coin collection his client had spent a lifetime acquiring.

Gift Giving in China

Strictly speaking, it is against the law . . . but the acceptance of gift giving is increasing.

1. Small gifts are customarily exchanged at first meetings as a way of saying "I hope this friendship will last."

2. Because gift giving is still a sensitive issue in China, avoid giving anything of any value in front of others. It could cause the recipient both embarrassment *and* trouble.

3. American businesspeople back from China generally agree that gift giving does little to improve business relations but that *not* giving can have a very negative effect.

4. There are two gifts that are perfectly legal and can be given openly. One is a banquet — your Chinese hosts will almost certainly give you one, and it is expected that you will return the favor. There is a very specific protocol to be followed. Banquets can be ordered at designated restaurants in four degrees of lavishness. The degree you choose must match the one your Chinese hosts chose for their banquet for you. Be sure that the restaurant you choose is acceptable to your guests and that the manager can advise you about making the right choice of banquet.

5. The other legal gift is a collective, symbolic gift from "your side to their side." It should be made clear by whoever presents the gift that it is on behalf of the whole group or company he represents and is meant for the whole group on the receiving end, although it must be handed to whoever is the acknowledged leader of the Chinese delegation.

6. Especially welcome on these occasions are gifts that commemorate the occasion or reflect the business you represent or the part of the country you come from.

7. Never give foreign currency in the People's Republic of China, not even commemorative coins if they have any exchange value.

8. Because there are few typewriters (Chinese characters are too numerous and complicated to fit on a keyboard), there is always an eager market for pens there. They sell inexpensive pens in nearly every kind of shop, but high-quality pens are a luxury any Chinese appreciates.

A banquet is a very acceptable gift in China.
But, be sure you arrange for the correct strata of banquet.

9. Do not give clocks. (In Chinese, the sound of the word sounds like the word for the prefuneral visit to the dying.)

10. Small personal mementos are appreciated more than lavish gifts that may cause embarrassment.

11. Kitchen gadgets, photo albums, name plaques for desk use, personally engraved pens, and records are especially popular. So is cognac.

12. All business negotiations should be completed before gifts of any value are exchanged.

13. On holidays, it is customary in Chinese cultures, including Taiwan, Singapore, and Hong Kong, for guests to give servants such as sweepers, maids, houseboys, etc., a small amount of local money in an envelope. In Hong Kong, red envelopes are available for this if you are there during the lunar New Year.

14. Do not bother wrapping a gift before you go through Customs, where it may be unwrapped. Simple wrappings or an attractive gift box are sufficient.

Explanatory Notes on Research for the Material on Gift Giving

In 1981, The Parker Pen Company commissioned Dr. Kathleen Kelley Reardon to research international gift-giving practices. Dr. Reardon is an associate professor of interpersonal and mass media communications in the Department of Communication Sciences at the University of Connecticut. Her specialization is in the area of persuasion and she has authored the book *Persuasion, Theory, and Context* (Sage Publications, 1981).

Because Dr. Reardon's research was an exploration into new territory, the reader may be interested in how it was conducted. Details on her methodology, along with more details on her findings, are explained here.

Basic Questions

The findings of this study may allow hypothesis testing in future studies. For this preliminary investigation, an exploratory approach was in order. The following research questions guided the exploration.

1. What do American businesspersons give as gifts in other regions of the world?

2. What are the characteristics of a good international business gift?

3. Do American businesspersons give differently in different regions of the world?

4. Does the style of giving influence the perception, selection, and presentation of gifts in other regions of the world?

5. Do American businessmen give differently from American businesswomen?

6. What are some of the concerns of American businesspersons when giving and receiving gifts in foreign lands?

The first five questions are answered by quantitative analyses of the data obtained from the telephone survey. The sixth question is addressed by qualitative analyses of the free response data gathered by both the telephone surveys and personal interviews.

The Subjects

The subjects for the telephone survey were primarily members of export councils throughout the United States, plus persons recommended by other subjects. The mean years of international business travel for these subjects was eighteen, suggesting a rather high level of expertise. Since this was a pilot study directed at locating the experts and beginning to assess their gift-exchange styles in other countries, we did not place emphasis on obtaining a random sample. However, to assure representation of U.S. regions, a random sample of export councils was used. Ninety-seven subjects from around the nation completed telephone interviews conducted by two researchers. Twenty-five Fortune 500 executives located in Connecticut, New York, and Washington, D.C., participated in face-to-face interviews.

Procedures

Two Ph.D. researchers contacted 200 international business executives by phone. The interviews took from 20 to 40 minutes. The typical interview took less than 35 minutes.

Ninety-seven respondents (eighty-eight men, nine women) completed the telephone survey. Only eighteen refused to participate. The others were away on business trips or otherwise unavailable. Twenty-five executives were personally interviewed. The face-to-face interviews were used to supplement the data obtained by phone.

Finally, interviews were conducted with several cultural anthropologists and with: Franchon Silberstein, director of the Overseas Briefing Center of the Foreign Service Institute; Gary Lloyd, director of the Business Council for International Understanding; Wallace Elton, senior vice president of the International Executive Services Corps; and other persons who engage in international business travel.

Methods

Data analysis took three forms. First, percentages were obtained for each response. Then more advanced analyses were conducted to assess differences in gift-giving styles among regions of the world, gender differences in gift giving, and the influence of gift-giving style on the types of gifts selected and the manner of gift presentation. Chi square, correlation, and analyses of variances were used where appropriate.

Survey Results

Research Question One: What do American businesspersons give as gifts in other regions of the world?

Subjects were asked, "What are some of the gifts you have given in other countries?" Table 1 provides a list of the most frequently mentioned gift items or types.

Table 1

Typical International Business Gifts

Gift Types	Percentage of Respondents Who Mentioned Giving These Gift Types
Unique items	53
Home and office decorations	51
Pens	50
Clothing	36
Liquor	31
Books and magazines	29
Electrical and computerized toys	24
Jewelry	21
Sports equipment and games	17
China and glassware	16
Knives and keychains	16
Food	10
Cologne or perfume	5

The analysis conducted to answer Research Question One indicated that the gifts American businesspersons give in other countries are, typically, distinctively American, useful, of conversational value, personalized or given with the recipient's personal preferences in mind, more often than not brand name items, and below $26 in cost. These gifts are intended as courtesy gifts more often than as strategic or personal gifts. Approximately one-third of the gifts described were logo items.

Research Question Two: What are the characteristics of a good international business gift?

Table 2

Importance of Primary Characteristics of the International Business Gift

Characteristic	Percentage Response		
	Not at all Important	Somewhat Important	Very Important
Distinctively American	5	36	59
Gift utility	20	43	37
Conversational value	16	52	32

Characteristic	Important	Not Important
Brand Name	56	44
Logo	36	64
Wrapping	49	51

Importance of typical price	Below $26	$26-$50	Above $50
	72	21	7

One of the telephone survey free-response questions also pertains to Research Question Two. Subjects were asked, "What characteristics should a business gift given in another country possess?" Table 3 provides the most prevalent responses.

Table 3

International Business Gift Characteristics

Characteristics	Percentage Response
Selected with the recipient or relationship in mind	41
Good quality or in good taste	37
Inexpensive or avoiding obligation	35
Representative of the United States	33
Unique or not easily obtainable in that country	30
Company or product reminder	29
Practical or useful	20
Small or lightweight	15

When describing their general gift-giving habits, many of the subjects indicated that they consider the recipient and the kind of relationship when selecting a gift. This is further supported by the fact that 83 percent of the subjects indicated that they personally chose the particular gift they described.

The subjects' spontaneous descriptions of gift characteristics also indicated that gifts should be of good quality but inexpensive, American, unique or unavailable in the recipient's country, a reminder of the company, practical or useful, and small or lightweight to facilitate transportation of the gift.

To determine whether the choice of gift was systematically related to the reason for giving, a series of analyses were conducted. Gift-giving intention was determined by a content analysis of responses to the question, "What did you want the gift to say?" The variable intention refers to the subject's intention when giving a particular gift he or she described. Responses were coded as strategic (emphasis on business goals), courtesy (emphasis on appropriateness), and personal (emphasis on appreciation of or interest in the relationship with the recipient). Two coders analyzed the responses. Initial intercoder agreement was 82 percent.

Table 4

Intention Behind International Business Gift Giving

Intention	Percentage Response
Courtesy	40
Strategic	38
Personal	22

Chi-square analyses indicate that the reason for giving (intention) is related to the type of gift selected. If American businesspersons wish to remind the recipient of the company (strategic intention), they usually select accessories or home and office decorations. Logo gifts are usually of this type. When selecting courtesy gifts, American businesspersons prefer perishable items and home and office decorations. The latter are not likely to be logo items but rather framed photographs, artwork, porcelain or glass figures, and other aesthetically appealing items.

Finally, when selecting a personal gift, the American businesspersons chose books, magazine subscriptions, and items unique to the recipient's tastes more often than other gifts. Unique items were primarily gifts known to be of value to the recipient. They may reflect a hobby, the style of the home, a compliment to intellectual interests, a recognition of a special interest, or an especially unusual conversation piece. Books and magazine subscriptions are also chosen with the recipient in mind. Books convey a message about the giver's perception of the recipient's taste in literature. Magazine subscriptions indicate that you know and appreciate the recipient's interests outside of business.

All gifts were coded as accessories, perishables, home and office decorations, books and magazines, unique gifts, or other gifts. The results of this coding procedure appear in Table 5.

Table 5

International Business Gift Types

Type	Percentage Response
Home and office decorations	27
Accessories	22
Unique gifts	18
Perishables	16
Books and magazines	10
Other	7

Chi-square analyses revealed that the three levels of intention (strategic, courtesy, and personal) and the six types of gifts are systematically related (p less than .0001). It appears that people consider the purpose of their gifts when selecting them. Accessories and home and office decorations are typical strategic gifts. Perishables (e.g., liquor) and home and office decorations were the most frequently mentioned courtesy gifts. And personal gifts were primarily books and magazines and unique gifts.

Research Question Three: Do American businesspersons give differently in different regions of the world?

To obtain this information, analyses of variance comparing three regions of the world (Japan and Taiwan, Latin America, and Western Europe) were conducted.* These analyses indicate that region affects the security with which the American businessperson gives a gift, the importance of conversational value, and the importance of the element of surprise.

It appears that Americans doing business in Japan are not as secure about the appropriateness of their gifts as they are in Western Europe. They are most secure in Latin America.

The fact that the subjects of this study felt more secure in their gift giving when in Latin America than when in Europe or Japan provides statistical support for the view of Latin gift giving expressed earlier in this report. The Latins enjoy gift giving. They like it for its own sake and for the meaning it conveys. Unlike in Japan, form is not of primary importance to them and the frequency of gift giving is not as foreign to the American businessperson. And unlike in Europe, gifts are not as status-related in Latin America, nor are the occasions for giving so limited. There is a comfort about gift giving and receiving in Latin America which implies that obligation is not the primary motivation; it is the thought that counts.

Finally, American businesspersons consider the element of surprise more important in Western Europe than in the Orient or in Latin America. Examination of these results demonstrates that surprise in gift giving is more important in Europe than in Latin America or Japan for a number of reasons. First, Orientals do not like to be surprised because they lose face if they are not prepared to reciprocate. Latin Americans, while enjoying surprise

---

*These were the three regions with a sufficiently large sample size to conduct analyses of variance.

more than the Japanese, expect gifts more than the Europeans. An alternative or supplementary explanation for the comparative preference for surprise in gift giving in Europe is that Americans perceive Europeans as more like themselves than are the Latin Americans and Japanese. Americans value surprise in gift giving and so may believe that others like them also appreciate surprise.

American businesspersons view conversational value as more important in the Orient than in Western Europe or Latin America.

According to Anna Chennault, lecturer, writer, and business consultant on the Orient, conversational value is far more important than utility in Japan. To the Japanese, gifts are so frequent and sometimes so meaningless that a gift which intrigues them is especially valuable. A former president of the Committee for Economic Development told our researcher that "the Japanese have to know what something is and how to use it." This implies both an appreciation for utility and insatiable curiosity. The latter may be the reason that conversational value is important.

An alternative explanation is that the Europeans prefer gifts with a personal touch or no gift at all. And the Latin Americans appreciate the personal message of the gift much more than any aspect of the gift itself. Thus, the Japanese, by comparison, appear more concerned with the conversational value of the gift, a perspective also evidenced by their brand-consciousness.

Wrapping Gifts

Chi-square analysis suggested that gift wrapping is especially important in Japan.

According to Dr. Howard Van Zandt, anthropologist and author of several books on Japan, wrapping gifts is very important in Japan because the Japanese people are very ceremonious and also generally prefer to avoid opening a gift in front of others. Gifts that are not wrapped place considerable pressure on the Japanese to pretend that they like a gift, even if they do not. The Japanese go to great lengths to avoid offense and to avoid creating situations in which some person may lose face.

It is also important to remember that the Japanese do not wrap gifts in the same manner as we do in the United States. It is not necessary that the American businessperson relinquish his ways of wrapping, but it is advisable to avoid ribbons unless aware of the various meanings they convey in terms of recipient status. Also, the bows used in the United States to decorate packages are generally unappealing to the Japanese. The safest route is to have gifts wrapped in Japan by those familiar with the customs.

Research Question Four: Does the type of giving influence the perception, selection, and presentation of gifts in other regions of the world?

General style of gift giving was determined by coding responses to the question, "What are some characteristics of a good international business gift?" into strategic, courtesy, or personal emphasis. This variable, unlike intention, refers to general giving style rather than to the style of giving peculiar to the one gift-giving event described by subjects earlier in the questionnaire. The results of this two coder procedure appear in Table 6. Initial intercoder agreement was 80 percent.

Table 6

International Business Gift-Giving Style

Style	Percentage Response
Courtesy	42
Personal	39
Strategic	19

Pearson correlation indicates that general giving style and perceived importance of gift conversational value are related (r .2576, p less than .05). The more personal the style, the more important the conversational value.

Perhaps thoughtful gifts are those which one may talk about more easily with others compared with those characterized by utility.

General giving is also related to the preference for giving or receiving. Responses to the question, "Do you agree with the statement, 'It is better to give than to receive'?" were compared to general giving styles. A chi-square analysis suggests that courtesy givers enjoy receiving as much as giving, but that both strategic and personal givers prefer giving to receiving (p less than .05).

The strategic givers interviewed in this study often explained their preference for giving in terms of their goals. One executive said, "I'm a seller. I don't expect to receive." Another said, "I'm marketing oriented. To me, being remembered is more important than receiving." And a senior vice president of a large Midwestern bank said, "(Giving) makes the other indebted to you and lays the groundwork for later business."

Courtesy givers responded much differently. One international businessman said, "It is better to give when you're receiving. It's worse to give and not receive; someone will lose face."

Several other courtesy givers described the gift exchange as a pleasurable activity. A president of a Midwestern company said, "It's always nice to get something back. But I don't ever remember expecting it." And a New Orleans executive explained, "The other should generally know about a gift in advance so that he might properly reciprocate." Another comment by this executive may explain the general tendency to prefer giving to receiving. He said, "Receiving a gift gracefully is much harder than giving."

Personal givers probably enjoy giving because they know the recipient well. Also, personal givers tend to do some research into the preference of their foreign counterparts. This should increase their confidence and pleasure in giving.

Research Question Five: Do American businessmen give gifts differently from American businesswomen?

Only 9 of the 97 telephone survey subjects in this investigation were women. This made most statistical analyses impractical. However, some differences between businessmen and businesswomen can be implied from comparisons of percentages. All of the women replied "no" when asked if the gift they had chosen to describe was a logo gift. Forty percent of the men had indicated that the gift they had chosen to describe was a logo gift.

All of the women had chosen the gifts themselves and 6 of the 9 had wrapped the gifts. Six of the 9 considered it "very important" that a gift be distinctively American. Seven of the 9 preferred giving to receiving. And, strategic giving was less frequent for females than for males.

Research Question Six: What are some of the concerns of American businesspersons when giving and receiving gifts in foreign lands?

Face-to-face interviews with 25 Fortune 500 international business executives provided the qualitative data needed to answer this question. Among the concerns expressed by these businessmen and women were (1) that the purpose of the gift might be misinterpreted; (2) the possibility of incurring obligation or becoming obligated by return gifts; (3) the possibility of embarrassing the recipient; (4) the possibility of unwittingly committing a cultural faux pas; and (5) determining what is appropriate given the nature of the relationship.

The delicate nature of intercultural gift exchange renders it an area of considerable concern to the American businessperson. Eighty-four percent of the telephone respondents and 100 percent of those interviewed in person for this study indicated that they could use a guide to international business gift exchange. This alone indicates that they are interested in knowing when and how to give and accept gifts in other countries.

Ninety-three percent of the telephone respondents indicated that they were at least somewhat sure that the one gift chosen to describe to the researcher was appreciated. However, in-person interviews and responses to several telephone survey questions indicate that confidence in gift giving and gift receiving is not high, even among the experienced businesspersons interviewed for this study. It appears that once the American businessperson has exhausted his or her limited repertoire of possible gifts, gift selection becomes a considerable challenge.

It is clear from this investigation that the potential for misperceptions of gift purpose is of considerable concern to American businesspersons working in other countries. Several respondents indicated that U.S. laws prohibiting the giving of large gifts have made everyone uncomfortable.

One manager of business development of a Fortune 300 company told our researcher, "I'm always worried about taking a gift that might be too much." Another executive explained, "Gift giving used to be a nice touch. But in some countries it is now a bribe. Gift giving has become a lost art in those countries." And a former U.S. ambassador said, "To keep gifts clearly gifts, the best thing to do is to make them personal, not ostentatious — and make them inexpensive." He added, "Monetary value and thought-fulness differentiate between bribes and gifts."

According to Marcel Mauss, author of *The Gift*, and Wilton Dillon, author of *Gifts and Nations*, a gift always incurs obligation. Despite the fact that 89 percent of the telephone interviewees believed that the gift they described did not incur obligation, study of the various cultures indicates that gifts incur some form of obligation everywhere. Perhaps obligation to repay in kind is not apparent, but repayment in some form is necessary if one values the relationship.

Businesspersons interviewed for this study were very concerned about incurring obligation if their purpose was courtesy giving or personal giving. Strategic givers often admitted that obligation is their purpose. One executive explained that gifts can "oil the skids along the way" in a business relationship. Another described gift giving as "good salesmanship."

The majority of respondents in this study did not describe their gift giving as intending to incur obligation. On the contrary, most seemed concerned that obligation might result despite their efforts to avoid it. The concern with incurring obligation and becoming obligated was expressed frequently by subjects of the study.

Saving Face

The concept of *face* has been given considerable attention in this study. There is not a region of the world where face is unimportant. The experienced international businessperson is aware of this fact. And so, one of his concerns is how to avoid embarrassing others. The way most commonly suggested by study respondents is to learn about other cultures before you visit them. Also, as one Fortune 500 executive suggested, "Make your gift giving a forethought rather than an afterthought." Another executive said, "Americans do a very bad job of gift giving." He explained that we don't bother to find out what is acceptable or unacceptable in other countries.

One of the telephone survey questions was, "How important is the element of surprise in international business gift giving?" Only 16 percent of the respondents considered it "very important." When asked why they did not consider it important, several said that surprise gifts can embarrass the recipient. He or she may not have something to give to you. In the Orient, this can cause loss of face — and a consequent loss of business.

Gift Timing

The timing of a gift presentation is as important as the gift itself. The Japanese like to give gifts when they meet others and also when they leave. In Europe, gift giving is a personal expression, and so the appropriate time is after the relationship has developed. In the People's Republic of China, gifts should be given only after the completion of business negotiations.

Despite these general rules, American businesspersons are not confident about the timing of gifts. One executive suggests, "Never initiate a gift exchange. Always let them give first." Another said, "It's always better to give when you receive. Then no one loses face." An American businesswoman suggests, "Whenever you give a gift to a man in a foreign country, a gift should be given to his wife as well." In France, a gift brought to the home should be given as soon as you arrive. In the People's Republic of China, personal gifts should not be given in front of others, whereas in the Arab countries, giving in front of others dispels the notion of a bribe and affords your host public esteem.

The Appropriate Gift

As far as gift appropriateness is concerned, it is clear from the responses that a gift must be relationship-appropriate as well as culturally appropriate. Since no two persons ever have exactly the same impression of any relationship, this is not an easy rule to follow. Also, American businesspersons find it difficult to think of a "distinctively American gift." Ninety-four percent of the respondents view this as at least somewhat important. And yet, as one subject said, "It is a real challenge to find a distinctively American gift." To assist the reader in meeting this challenge, we have compiled the following list of distinctively American gifts derived from subject responses.

Maple syrup
U.S. stamps
Stetson hats
American sports equipment
Pen or desk set with
  company or state insignia
American magazine
  subscription
Cigarettes
Mugs
M&Ms
Road atlas
Western belt buckles
T-shirts from U.S. colleges
Liberty bell miniatures
Latest in children's
  electronic toys
Macadamia nuts
  (Hawaii)

American Indian art or jewelry
Photo books of America or state
Sunflower pins (Kansas)
Records (e.g., Boston pops, jazz)
Pennsylvania Dutch items
Oreo cookies
Steuben glass
Scrimshaw
Gold-plated aspen leaves
  (Colorado)
U.S. coins
California wines
U.S. calendars
U.S. regional art
Peanut butter
Tool sets
Grand Canyon paper-
  weights
Framed photos of a region or
  historic site

One executive told this researcher, "Anyone who doesn't give gifts is missing out on an important part of business." One of the reasons for his view was his belief in the remembrance value of gifts. When asked why verbal sentiment is insufficient, several businesspersons mentioned the lasting memory value of gifts.

Verbal thought is soon lost. A gift emphasizes and perpetuates the idea. Manager of business development, Fortune 500 oil company.

Words don't last as long as something tangible. Circumstances often make it embarrassing to say "thank you." Vice president for international business development, Fortune 500 company.

The words "thank you" are overused and commonplace. The art of sincere communication has been obscured. Vice president for Latin America, Midwestern company.

For the same reason that books aren't tape-recorded — retention value. Pens are good because you use them often. A reminder of your company may tip a business decision in your favor. Vice president of business development, Fortune 500 company.

These responses suggest that to err in gift giving can negatively influence the success of business negotiations — especially in world regions where gift giving is a social requirement. Although respondents to this study expressed pride in being American, 97 percent affirmed that they believe we should adjust to other cultures. One president of a major international marketing company said, "I'm a great believer that an American business-man should be an ambassador of goodwill from his country. Unfortunately, that is not usually the case." The international businesspersons personally interviewed were of one mind on the adjustment to other cultures: it is a necessary part of doing business.

Conclusion

One Fortune 500 vice president of international business explained, "There is no greater gift than information." Dr. Wilton Dillon, director of seminars at the Smithsonian Institute, explained to our researcher that the United States is most generous with its information. We give to other countries, often without expectation of recompense. Here, Dr. Dillon says, is where we make our mistake. The one who gives must allow the recipient to repay. To do otherwise is to place the recipient in an inferior position while the giver basks in the superiority derived from generosity.

The preference for giving over receiving is understandable but likely to elicit resentment rather than gratitude. People must be allowed to give as well as receive. The exchange need not be equitable in monetary terms, but there must be a satisfactory exchange. The perception of equality in gift exhange from the viewpoint of both parties must be present, or at least possible, for a relationship to survive.

This is where the American businessperson experiences a dilemma. Receiving is not comfortable for Americans. This American preference for giving is one of the primary reasons for the businessperson's discomfort with gift exchanges in his own and other cultures.

The second obstacle is the fact that we belong to an individualistic culture rather than to an associative culture. We have mobility. More often than not, we are born and reared in families consisting of fewer than six people. Unlike the Japanese, we are not crowded. On the contrary, we expect to have our space. In contrast to the Arabs, we marry whomever we choose to marry and our occasional blunders bring shame to ourselves rather than to an entire family. Moreover, we do not win praise for our generosity so much as for our personal accomplishments. To the Arab, reciprocity is a way of life and there is no self without others, for it is they who define the self.

The Latin American male puzzles us because he expresses his affection without compromising his masculinity. He does not depend on his wife to select and present gifts in the proper fashion. And he does not measure a gift by its monetary value. He measures others by their sincerity and their potential as friends. He is not embarrassed by requests for assistance and takes great pleasure in assisting his friends.

Even the Europeans challenge our comprehension by their insistence on propriety in gift giving. A gift is a personal expression, one that must be carefully thought through and performed with the utmost suavity. A gift in Europe must be considerably more than a gesture or it is nothing at all, a liability rather than an asset to your reputation as a businessperson.

And, finally, it is of some concern to us that our gifts given in the People's Republic of China can cause the loss of face. Should this occur, we might as well pack up our briefcases and head home. The gift, the timing of its presentation, and the mode of presentation must not be treated lightly in any country, especially in China. The Chinese are a people preoccupied with form.

Americans are unique in their emphasis on self. This perspective makes it difficult for Americans to comprehend and appreciate the ceremonious nature of the Japanese, his response to crowded conditions, and his view of self as part of a large unit. The gift escalation tendencies of the Arabs as a means of winning praise offend the American's sensibilities. The European seems aloof in his insistence on propriety, and the Chinese seems curiously hesitant to trust, while the Latin American comes on a bit too strong.

All of this can be offensive to the person who cannot relate to cultural differences by transcending the boundaries of his or her own customs and mores. This study suggests that above all others, this transcendence of one's cultural barriers presents the greatest challenge to the American who wants to conduct his business in foreign lands.

The second challenge is to define for oneself the meaning of a gift. It is important for Americans to separate a gift from a bribe in their own minds. One Fortune 500 vice president of personnel said, "If there is no compromise of business or personal interests by either party in the exchange, it is a gift." Perhaps this comes closer than other attempts to define what a gift *is not*. What a gift *is* can only be determined by the members of the exchange. At least two persons contribute to the definition of any gift and the intended message is not always the one received.

The third challenge is to admit to ourselves that gift giving is rarely, if ever, an act of disinterested generosity. Only then can we understand and appreciate the need others have to give to us. Despite the religious ideas that exalt pure giving, studies of cultures indicate that it is not common to human societies.

It is a source of some concern that 89 percent of the telephone survey respondents thought that the gift they chose to describe for the study did not incur obligation on the part of the recipient. From readings of literature on the subject of giving, it is clear to us that all gifts incur some kind of obligation to some degree. Gifts incur obligation because human beings all over the world require, at the very least, some form of equity in their relationships. Otherwise, as George Homans suggests, they "incur inferiority." The businessman you cause to feel inferior can never consider himself an equitable business counterpart — or a friend. It is wise for Americans to recognize that a gift, in fact, obligates — even if it obligates differently in each culture and each relationship. One-sided or unbalanced generosity in a business relationship does much more harm than good.

The American businessman who can understand that gift giving is a form of persuasion — which, in fact, incurs obligation and cries for balance in the give-and-receive equation — will be in a much better position than others to bridge some of the cultural gaps described in this study. The chances of his gifts being appreciated — and business negotiations moving forward — will be much greater.

CHAPTER 4

American Jargon
and
Baffling Idioms

International misunderstandings,
or
Why a German understands a Japanese speaking English, but neither may understand an American

U.S. industry sends forth thousands of emissaries each year, confident that wherever they take their act their language is sure to be spoken. Too bad so many forget to ask, but will it be *understood*? That blissful indifference has created a modern-day "Tower of Business Babel."

American business is one of the worst offenders in language proliferation. Imagine the confusion of your overseas business contact when on one trip he meets the Personnel Director only to find on the next visit that person is now called (as is the growing custom) Director of Human Resources. Same with the fellow in charge of insurance; he is now Director of Risk Management. American business has created *two* types of auditors: internal and external. And if you are still not convinced, try to find someone who calls himself (or herself) a "salesperson." They are now all "account managers" or "service representatives."

The way the mother tongue trips from our lips these days — tintinnabulating with buzzwords, cusswords, puns, gags, technical and business jargon, sports and military metaphors, show biz zingers, hyperbole, euphemisms, Latinisms, and all the other isms from local to colloquial — is it any wonder that it ends up sounding like Greek to everyone else?

Ambiguity's price can be steep, far costlier than a lost laugh or a dent in the conversational flow. Why should a Saudi purchasing agent buy from an American whose English he finds unfathomable, when the same language as spoken by a French or Japanese salesman comes across loud and clear?

Communications Crisis

A questionnaire on the subject of international communications was completed by 204 corporate executives, business owners, consultants, trainers, bankers, and other movers and shakers with high mileage in overseas trade. *It is clear that America faces a communications crisis that neither Berlitz nor bytes alone can solve.* Fully 80 percent of these business travelers reported difficulties conducting business with foreigners because of the latter's misunderstanding of American English. They also pointed out that the answer lies with us — not with technology. In other words, if the message is not clear, the media cannot help.

Let's deal first with our sins, then with our salvation as suggested by the tips and cautionary tales from these respondents.

The Seven Deadliest Sins
of International Misunderstanding

Local color

Jargon

Slang

Officialese

Humor

Vocabulary

Grammar

Local Color: From Idioms to Accents

As nervous as a long-tailed cat
in a room full of rocking chairs.

A memorable way to make your point, perhaps —unless your audience has never seen a rocking chair. We tend to take the fixtures of our American culture, from rockers to home runs, for granted. As a result, the word pictures we Americans paint are often seen by others as a jumble of foreign objects.

Flat as a pancake
Safe as Fort Knox
Old as Methuselah
Funny as a rubber crutch

. . . and clear as mud to a citizen of Peru or the Punjab. Even when all the words are familiar, the figure of speech itself can be baffling, even insulting.

Raining cats and dogs
Flying by the seat of your pants
Coming up roses
Don't make waves
Keep a low profile

Most of us do not stop to realize how many of our metaphors come right off the playing field — and not Eton's but the Astrodome's. No matter how avid a golfer or baseball fan your foreign counterpart is, American sports terminology is still likely to leave him out in left field.

Asking for a ballpark figure rarely gets you to first base. Aces, end runs, slam dunks, and playing for all the marbles are not worldwide business maneuvers. One U.S. firm lost a client simply by remarking, "This is a whole new ball game." The client did not consider the discussion a game. But then, how would you cope with a Spaniard who habitually laced his replies with bullring terms? "Excuse me, señor, but I must do a *paso double* to your proposal."

Bonjour, tristesse

Once the tongue of diplomats, courtesans, and other dignitaries, French has, *helas*, fallen on sad times. For Americans, at least, it is now mere punctuation: *Mon dieu! Zut alors! Entre nous. Chacun à son gout . . .*

It's not that we lack perfectly good English to say the same thing. But there will always be those (or as Miss Piggy would say, "But surely, sweets, not *moi!*") who feel the urge to Frenchify. If this is one of your weaknesses, better not give in to it when on the road. Especially on la rue. Lovers of the language (including most educated Europeans, North Africans, and other peoples colonized by the French) hate the way we pronounce it. And nonlovers of the language will neither know nor care what all the *entre nous*es and *son gout*s are about.

Hail, Caesar

One of the oldest languages is also one of the latest to invade the conference room. Not even the mailroom boy seems able to keep the *per se*s, *ad hoc*s, and *quid pro quo*s out of his syntax.

A touch of Latin can make a weak-kneed sentence sound more authoritative, perhaps. But unless your field is religion or the law, there are good English equivalents— and good reasons to use them. One, you don't risk the usual misusages and over-usages. Two, you don't embarrass the Japanese engineer who spent twenty years mastering English but, unsurprisingly, still does not know an *id est* from an *a priori*. Three, you don't look silly to the English stenographer who was translating *The Aeneid* while the rest of us were sounding out Dr. Seuss.

"Look Ali, if you folks will play ball with my team, we can split home-run profits with double play efficiency . . ."

There are many Latin words embedded in our language which we *cannot* do without. Yet they still have not become Anglicized enough to be treated like regular English; for example, media, data, algae, stimulus, curriculum — et cetera. There's no danger they will be misunderstood by others, but big danger they will be misspoken by *us*.

All too few executives appear to be aware that the singular of media is not media — or that the plural of curriculum is not just a matter of adding an *s* — or that data takes a plural verb, not an "is" or a "was." But never mind if you never took Latin I. Just find someone who did and ask for a crash course in endings. (Total semester time: about ten minutes.)

When in Rome, then, do not necessarily say what the Romans say — or said. Also, do not necessarily say what you say at home. And that goes for the *way* you say it as well.

Ciao to all that

Down-home accents and word variations can be incomprehensible even to someone well-versed in standard American as pronounced by television commentators and language instructors. For instance, a Texas businessman reports that an innocent "y'all" got him into hot water right in his own backyard. When he urged his client from overseas, "Y'all come for another visit," the visitor interpreted it to mean he should return with more people next time.

Still another "y'all" invitation, this one in Jedda, insulted the sheiks it was meant for, because they assumed it included their subordinates.

Beware of drawls and twangs. They may be colorful, but they can make the simplest syllable come out like a trombone note dipped in motor oil ("caay-yunt" for "can't"), while big-city talk often chews words up and spits them out like day-old Bazooka gum ("wadja" for "what did you").

Even after you tame the accent, remember: *not too fast and not too slow*. Fast is hard to grasp and slow is patronizing. "You can actually judge an American's experience in export," claims one corporate officer, "by the rate of his speech."

Repetition doesn't hurt, either. As the old Madison Avenue adage goes, "Tell 'em what you're gonna tell 'em. Tell 'em. Then tell 'em what you told 'em." It sells a lot of cornflakes, and it works on a lot of non-Americans who would rather miss your point than lose face admitting they missed it.

Ordinary Language

The editor of this book traveled with a small group of Americans to the People's Republic of China in 1976. Included in the group was a famous trademark attorney. One evening the Chinese took the two of us aside and said, "We need your advice. One of you has experience in consumer goods, the other in registering trademarks. We wish to sell our sewing machines in America and would like your reaction to the brand name we have chosen."

"What name do you want to use?" asked the Americans.

"We want to call it," said the Chinese with great pride, "the 'Ordinary Sewing Machine.'"

We Americans could not help wincing. To our careful queries into why they had chosen the name "ordinary," the Chinese officials explained, "That is the direct translation from our language. Besides, in our country with our classless society, it is a good term. Why? Is it bad in America?"

"Yes," we answered. Ordinary, we explained, meant "common," and they would do better to call their machine the "Supremo" or the "Premier." This clearly troubled the Chinese, and after a night of contemplation, they returned in the morning with this puzzled rejoinder.

"You remember you said that 'ordinary' was a bad word for a brand name in American because it meant 'common'?"

We remembered.

"How is it, then, that in America you have The Standard Oil Company?"

One piece of advice comes from a lady with a dog-eared passport and a VP on her letterhead. "Speak to the rest of the world," she says, "as if answering a slightly deaf, very rich old auntie who just asked you how much to leave you in her will."

In at least one culture, the Japanese, *silence* is an important aspect of clear communications. Americans abhor silence; those gaps must be filled. But among the Japanese, it is common — even expected — to have periods of silence in which the Japanese businessman contemplates what has been said. The Japanese cannot understand why an American dislikes those quiet moments. As one Japanese businessman asked, "Do American businesspeople think and talk at the same time?"

Finally, keep in mind that your English-as-a-second-language business counterpart may take your words quite literally. One Midwestern executive sent a cable to his Peruvian manager saying, "Send me factory and office headcount broken down by sex." The reply came, "249 in factory, 30 in office, 3 on sick leave, none broken down by sex — our problem is with alcohol."

Jargon: The tongue without a brain

Why think when you can just talk? Jargon is to communication approximately what painting by numbers is to art. Somebody else works out the logistics, then we take our little kit and dab the colors in the appropriate spaces. An "input" here. A "feedback" there. "Bottom lines" everywhere.

Is there anyone among us who hasn't met the systems analyst who lost the power to say anything but "interface" the year the silicon chip was invented? Too bad for those nice old pensioned-off words that used to do the job — "share," "coordinate," "work together," "common ground" — all forced into early retirement as soon as the upstart grabbed the reins. But wait. Interface's number will soon be up, for it is in jargon's very genes to die a sudden and unmourned death. (Remember when not even a salami was worth a second glance unless it was "state of the art"?)

The trick is to detect the moment when those vital signs begin to falter. Using yesterday's buzzword today ("buzzword" currently being everyone's favorite buzzword) is as fatal a career move as rolling a hoola hoop to the office.

Words to be wariest of are those with a high-tech heritage, since they keep changing as quickly as the industry that hatches them. On the other hand, terms from such notably low-tech spheres as banking and advertising have been around so long even a Kazakstani could probably read you. That does not guarantee, however, that the Englishman next to him could, too.

> *On the same wave length*
> *Shotgun approach*
> *Overview*
> *Run it up the flagpole*
> *Downtime*
> *Wallpaper the meeting*
> *100K (for 100,000)*
> *Sandbag*
> *It will never fly*
> *Dog and pony show*
> *On a roll**

Understanding them depends on how many jet-stream Willy Lomans your overseas contacts have encountered. So why not avoid following in Willy's footsteps altogether? Put it as only you can put it. Not only will it sound much more sincere, but searching for your own words crystalizes the whole thought, while clichés allow the sentences to slip off your tongue causing scarcely a blip on your EEG.

Please remember, though, that *all* esoterica is not jargon. Every profession has its own insider language for which there is no legitimate substitute. Even if it is changing every nanosecond, there is nothing trendy or slangy about this kind of terminology. A regional manager in the communications industry cites a few examples he is currently coping with.

> *Frequency hopping*
> *Spread spectrum*
> *Shake, rattle, roll*
> *SNAPS technology*
> *System architecture*

Whether you take your business lexicon as far as Lima, Ohio, or Lima, Peru, never assume even your opposite number there knows what you are talking about. An American representing his company on a swing through West Germany tells of breezing through a description of a heat-treating process called pickling. The German interpreter stopped him short and grabbed a dictionary. Nonetheless, the best German equivalent she could offer her obermeisters was *gurke*. So instead of "pickling," they got "cucumber."

---

*Not from the hot dog industry but a sporticism meaning running like Herschel Walker through the business world.

A "dog and pony show" is not a dog and pony show.

Coast-speak

A lot of pin-striped jargon may have gone to Harvard Business School, but all the more unbuttoned manifestations of the form took the red-eye in direct from the Coast. (There is only one Coast, incidentally, and it is not the North, South, or East one.)

Cradle of high-tech, California has also given us that socio-and psycho-babble into which even the squarest of us lapse when not fiercely vigilant or entirely sober.

Friendships, love affairs, even lifelong loathing no longer exist. Instead, there are "relationships." When somebody says he wants to "share" something with you, he is referring not to his wine or his wife but the story of his life. California, of course, is where long ago someone invited a few friends over to grump about a dull job or a philandering spouse and had the genius to call it consciousness raising. (A whole new industry was born.) Now, any get-together with a serious agenda such as politics, foreplay, or macrobiotic mulching is a workshop. To use such terms outside the privacy of your own hot tub is bad taste. To use them outside the *country* is positively xenophobic.

Yet another California product that travels fast but not well is the verb. Anyone within five Ferrari lengths of Rodeo Drive "takes" a meeting, "does" drugs (or carrot juice or *some*thing), and above all "flows." This last denotes the much envied ability to stay cool even if one's six-figure contract just blew out to Catalina. Whatever you claim on a conference call to L.A. (*never* Los Angeles, of course), let it not be that you are "laid back" or you will hear nothing but clicks on the other end. The phrase-of-the-day is "kicked back," though what it will be by the time this line comes back from the printer, who knows?

General Confusion in Command

"Reentry," "burnout," "abort," "jettison," etc., have all been given new life — and new meaning — by the military. Once a word has been to Mars, not many earthlings will forget its meaning. But what most of us do trip over is that Space-Shuttle-to-Command-Central habit of calling a spade not a spade but a "facility" or "mode" or some other Houstonized nonword that requires half a dozen more before anyone knows what is going on. A facility can, in fact, be anything from the launchpad to the space arm to the head.

Businesspeople have taken to this not *double*talk but *quin-tuple*talk like astronauts to moon dust. Words become phrases, phrases paragraphs, and your audience paralyzed. Nothing loses a foreign ear faster than a parade of modifiers struggling to do what the subject of the sentence should have done in the first place. In short, call a toilet a toilet — not a "relief facility."

Slang: Leapin' Lizards or —— You?

Whether you are a folksy cusser or a four-letter one, the time for slang of any kind is *never* during business hours. Even if the scene is dinner or drinks and the company the oldest of friends, chances of misinterpretation are too great. A "geewhillikers" kind of remark, even in London, often simply draws a blank, while a saltier phrase, however amicably intended, may easily be misread as a serious insult.

In Islamic and Buddhist cultures, a mere "thank God" is taken as blasphemy unless unmistakably meant piously, while any interjection with sexual overtones will surely bring the wrath of Allah down on you. But religious strictures aside, there is always the risk of coming off as too casual, nervy, or disrespectful.

The You Nobody Knows

What happens when the last briefcase is snapped shut and your hosts invite you out on the town? Do you remain Mary Poppins or do you let King Kong out of the cage?

Often when business seems to be officially over, it is actually just beginning. Your overseas hosts expect you to relax and reveal a little more of the real you. In fact, that may be the whole point. The rollicking businessman's binge is a standard tactic, especially in Japan, for sizing up the other side. Whether at the conference table, on the golf course, or in a geisha house, avoid any expletives you may regret the next morning. Remember that even if he was not at the party, the top man you are dealing with is very much aware that *you* were.

One U.S. traveler recalls good-naturedly dropping a few X-rated monosyllables while out with a Malaysian customer, who a few days later turned inexplicably surly. The problem? Without understanding its precise implications, the Malay had taken a fancy to one of the American's zingers and later had sprung it on one of his own customers, who did, indeed, understand. Bad news for both East *and* West.

It isn't just expletives that can get you into trouble, either. We forget that many of our slangiest expressions have had the four-letter words bleeped out of them (as in "mother" and "hit the fan"). But if your audience has not forgotten, the effect will be much

"Change the order. American says 'scratch the potatoes.'"

harsher than you intended. The same goes for words that, over here, may seem perfectly bland (as in "smart ass") but in different surroundings can be quite shocking. Even "belly up," according to several Americans back from overseas, invariably draws snickers or blank stares.

Avoid the usual ephemera such as "with it," "go for it," and "no way," not only because they are unimaginative to begin with but also because they are old hat before the rest of the world has ever heard them. Even slang that has survived for generations may still have never left the country.

Another innocent abroad gave his order in a Japanese restaurant, then changed his mind and called the waiter back. "Scratch the sushi," he said. The sushi was, of course, promptly served — presumably properly scratched, as ordered.

Officialese: Shorter is Not Always Clearer

"Found under carnal knowledge," the legendary charge brought against Elizabethan adulterers (though actually coined at the start of *this* century), inspired the world's first acronym to really catch on. Still the most popular of them all, it is now daddy to a huge litter of late-20th-century progeny.

From MASH, MERV, and MOMA to CAD/CAM, FYI, ASAP, and SWAK, civilization takes great pride in squeezing a few self-explanatory words into a squat chunk of capital letters, which take on a life of their own so fast that the words they stand for shrivel and fall away like husks from autumn corn. Maybe it is all part of progress and conservation —shorter words, fewer pages, less deforestation.

But unless everybody knows what you are shortening, the best policy is length — even if you have to spell out ILGWU or ASCAP. If nothing else, it serves to remind *us* what we are talking about.

The same goes for abbreviations such as R&R and P&L and C.E.O., which are basic English to us, alphabet soup to everyone else. Only when you are referring to the same thing over and over is it safe to revert to initials.

Humor: One Man's Mede is Another Man's Persian

Just don't try out S. J. Perelman's famous pun on an Iranian, for one culture's dazzling wordplay is another's dud. If gorgonzola can cross vast oceans, why can't a joke make it safely across 42nd Street without curdling?

Because humor is an acquired — and very perishable — taste. While to a Frenchman, the essence of humor is an aphorism from La Rochefoucauld, nine out of ten Americans think La Rochefoucauld is goat cheese. Not that anyone arrives in Hong Kong cracking "flied lice" jokes or in Poznan asking, "How many Poles does it take . . ." But truly tasteless jokes are not the only yuks to leave at home.

Humor need not stalk the streets in a ski mask to alienate aliens. Mots dressed up in banker's gray and academic tweeds are just as unwelcome at border crossings. Puns, double entendres, irony, sarcasm, Oscar Wilde, Dorothy Parker, and Johnny Carson remain unexportable.

I Never Mediterranean I Didn't Like

Ha ha. Except in the Mediterranean. Ethnic slurs can be detected where you never meant them. Affecting an accent like your host's, for example, though intended as a friendly joke or even as a compliment, will almost certainly be taken as an insult. Never try to get a chuckle at the expense of the national cuisine or architecture or government. And although it is safe for the locals to ridicule their own traffic jams and smog and the plumpness of their women, these are not for us to notice, much less crack wise about.

Or, as an Atlantan who covers the world for his securities firm reminds us, "If there is one thing that isn't funny in a foreign country, it's humor." Yours, that is.

Vocabulary and Grammar: Right Idea/Wrong Word

Most English-speaking foreigners with whom we deal are at the mercy of a limited vocabulary and rudimentary sentence structure. Yet the English they can speak is frequently more technically correct than ours! After all, they were taking lessons long after we parsed our last sentence in sixth grade. They wouldn't dream of dangling a participle or misplacing a modifier, while we break so many rules that we have come to speak a broken English all our own. We understand it, but does anyone else?

The American who says "infer" when he means "imply" leaves his listeners stumped, not because of what they *don't* know but because they do know the words have exactly opposite meanings.

They also know that "hardly," "scarcely," and "barely" are negatives themselves and therefore never belong with a "not." So when the American says, "I couldn't read hardly a word of your contract," his listeners breathe a sigh of relief. Unbeknownst to himself, he has just told them he had no trouble at all with the contract.

Word-wise, Sentence Foolish

Anybody with a few English lessons under his belt can tell you what "wise" means — except when you tack it onto another word, as in, "Diesel-wise, this machine outperforms everything else on the road." A wise diesel? Maybe your customer would rather have a dumb but reliable one.

Another factor contributing volumes to international misunderstanding is our native exuberance. Call something "fantastic" or "fabulous" and an unsuspecting foreigner may think you mean unreal or imaginary. To us, a disaster can be anything slightly less than perfect ("Lunch was a disaster — they ran out of fresh chives"). People on other continents think of disaster as pestilence, war, famine, and death.

We also tend to overdramatize both friend and foe with descriptions like "idiot," "clown," "slave driver," and "prince." Again, we forget that our audience only knows what they read in their pocket dictionary.

Don't Ask for the Little Girl's Room in Minsk

The other side of the too-graphic coin is not-nearly-graphic-enough. Why is a nation of pioneers and log splitters terrified of the word toilet? "Bathroom," "rest room," "powder room," "comfort station" — all are likely to be taken literally by foreigners, who will tell you, "Sorry, but we don't have one of those." Say that you want to "wash up" and you may be given a hot towel. Calling a toilet a toilet is particularly useful when making hotel reservations, because even in Paris, many hotel rooms, though almost always equipped with a sink (and even a bidet), do not have a toilet closer than the end of the hall.

All the words we use should be simple and straightforward, not just the touchy ones. And, above all, make sure *you* understand them before springing them on alien ears. In a schedule of events at a petroleum convention in Houston, it was announced, "Alumni from all United States universities can conjugate and sit together . . ." Foreign delegates who checked the meaning of conjugate in the dictionary no doubt spent the afternoon in the bar.

Sentences should be not only short and simple but almost audibly punctuated. You can't say a comma or a semicolon unless you are Victor Borge, but you can use pauses and full stops to break up each thought into chewable bits the same way dots and dashes do.

Looks like it's going to rain "cats and dogs."

Me Tarzan You Jane

Simplicity can, of course, be overdone. Never go on to the next point until the last one is thoroughly understood. But never speak condescendingly, either. When pausing to ask if your listeners got it, either do it lightly ("It's a complicated subject. Did I go too fast?") or put the onus on yourself ("Sometimes I speak too quickly. Shall I go over that again?")

No matter how wide a communication gap you face, you will never bridge it sounding like a teacher of enunciation.

Other Languages, Other Misunderstandings

Our own language may be a pesky traveling companion, but when we get where we're going we are in for even more problems. Foreign usages have a way of sabotaging the best-laid English sentence — even in England.

For instance, the general manager of his firm's international division tells of complimenting a distinguished English gentleman on the knickers he was wearing. Why did the gentleman turn crimson? In Britain, knee-length trousers are called "plus fours," while "knickers" are ladies' underpants.

Misunderstandings flow the other way, too. When an Englishman says that the project will be finished "at the end of the day," he simply means that it will be done when it's done — which could take six months. Even a word as unambiguous as "backlog" can convey the wrong impression. To the British, a large backlog implies not a wonderful list of orders waiting to be filled but a hopelessly overstocked inventory someone was too inefficient to move off the shelves. Much to the surprise of a Magnavox representative at a London meeting, when he suggested "tabling" the next item on the agenda his host immediately began to discuss it; the verb turns out to have the opposite meaning over there. Tell a Londoner you want to "fill him in," and he thinks you are going to hit him over the head. Say, "My presentation bombed" in America and you mean, of course, that it failed. In London, the term "bomb" means just the opposite — a great success.

Innocent little words can trip you up in Spanish-speaking countries as well. "Discuss," for example, sounds like the Spanish word *discutir*, which presupposes disagreement and hence connotes that you want to argue rather than just plain discuss. "Support" often strikes the Spanish sensibility as hinting at financial aid — not a wise commodity to ask a client or a government official to lend you. In case you do say the wrong thing, do not try to say you are embarrassed in what seems like proper Spanish — *Estoy embarazado*. It means you are pregnant.

On the other hand, when a Frenchman "demands" something, no offense should be taken. The French verb for ask is *demander*. And when he says "actual" he probably means what the word means in French: "at present."

The word that gets Americans in Japan into the most trouble is "you." To a Japanese, it is almost a violation of his territory — like jabbing a finger under his nose. At the very highest levels, Japanese businessmen do not expect to be addressed directly or even *looked* at directly. Those whom you deal with at other levels do not think in terms of self but of company. "What do *you* think?" is not the point. What the *company* thinks is.

Another Oriental phobia is "no." There is no real "no" in the Japanese language. Instead, there is a kind of unpleasant hiss or sad-faced "It is very difficult." If you ask, "Do you want any spares?" do not settle for less than, "No, I do not want any spares." If you end a question by asking, "No?" the Japanese says, "Yes," meaning, "Yes, I meant no." In other words, he is saying that yes, he understands, not yes, he'll comply.

Lastly, even unsuspecting words can spring traps. An American told his Japanese customer, "Our thinking is in parallel." The Japanese agreed, but after many months nothing happened. Frustrated, the American asked, "Why didn't you act? We agreed our thinking was in parallel." The Japanese responded, "Yes, but I looked the word parallel up in the dictionary and it said 'two lines that never touch.'"

Interpreting Interpreters

Why struggle to make yourself understood when you can hire a multilingual whiz to do it for you?

As discussed in an earlier section, handing your thoughts over to someone else to express can be as risky as letting a backseat driver reach over your shoulder and do the steering. Does he know exactly where you want to go? And is he seeing the road from the same perspective you are? Unless you have been doing your act together for a long time, it is hard to tell.

A more or less correct translation of your *words* can badly betray your *sentiments*. "Can you give me your answer today?" isn't very different from "Give me your answer today" — yet one sounds reasonable, the other pushy and demanding. Expressing a question by the intonation of your voice ("These are your lowest estimates?") does not guarantee that it will come out a question in the other language.

If you are using technical language of any kind, even just normal business terms such as "Xerox," "stat," "round figure," or "blue pencil," do not depend on a professional interpreter to know the proper translation. Also, do not expect him/her to admit to not knowing. Like everybody else, they are paid for what they know, not for what they have to look up in the dictionary.

Nor is it possible for most Americans to tell how an interpreter sounds to the other side. For instance, if he is from Spain, his standard Castilian Spanish will probably strike an Argentine or Mexican as "too Spanish" and hence daunting — like a Cockney being lectured by someone with an Oxbridge accent. And the accent of a Latin American can grate on a Castilian's ear like a snapped guitar string. The French, too, are supersensitive to regional French accents. A Parisian may have an adverse reaction to a Toulouse translator without even being conscious of it.

So Whom Can You Trust?

Beware interpreters provided by the other side. Not that they are deliberate saboteurs, but it is only human to harbor a bias in favor of one's own employer. They may instinctively overlook nuances that express urgency, irritation, or even diffidence. Particularly in the Far East, where the urge to please submerges most other motivations, your go-between is likely to be reluctant to carry a message for you.

And, should you be lucky enough to discover the mistranslation before it is too late, how can you complain when the translator is your client's right-hand man?

One director of his company's international trade division hit on a solution. First he created a new title: corporate interpreter. Then he gave the job to a young Japanese studying for his Ph.D. over here. Not only was the Oriental's English nearly flawless, but he was ambitious enough to master both the technical side of the company *and* its corporate culture. "He is no mere set of vocal chords," says the director proudly; "he's a business consultant."

Traveling Checklist

1. **The eyes have it.** Keep a constant lookout for the glazed expression and the wandering or sleepy eye that tells you that you have lost your audience.

2. **"Is that perfectly clear?"** Don't guess, ask. Nods and smiles do not necessarily signify understanding.

3. **Stop and start.** Don't wait until the end of a speech or even a sentence before checking for comprehension. Never go on to B until A is thoroughly grasped.

4. **Spot quiz.** Don't take yes for an answer. Ask probing questions that prove how much your listener is really absorbing.

5. **After office hours.** If possible, meet with your opposite number for a quiet one-on-one double check of understanding on both sides.

6. **Shortcut shortcuts.** Avoid "i.e.," "ditto," "etc.," etc. Say "we will" instead of "we'll" and "I believe your proposal is not acceptable" instead of "I don't believe your proposal is acceptable."

Plus These Quickies

- Enunciate distinctly and slowly.
- Overpunctuate with pauses and full stops.
- Make one point at a time, one sentence at a time.
- Paraphrase and ask others to do the same.
- Avoid questions that can be answered yes or no.
- If there is a misunderstanding, take the blame.
- Use visual aids (photos, sketches, diagrams, graphs).
- Use both languages in visual presentations like flip charts, videotapes, and slide shows.
- Put what you are going to say in writing *before* you say it.
- Write and distribute a report on what was said as soon as possible after the meeting.
- Never use numbers without writing them out for all to see.
- If possible, say numbers in both languages.
- Send a follow-up telex and/or letter to confirm what was said by telephone.
- Let your host set the pace of negotiations.
- Greet foreigners in their language, especially if it is an uncommon one like Arabic, Urdu, and Hindi.
- In Japan, learn terms of greeting and departure phonetically so you will be understood.
- Take a foreign-language cassette with you to practice pronunciation as you go along.
- Do not speak whole sentences in a language you have not thoroughly mastered.
- One exception to the above: "Where is the toilet?".

- Never interrupt.
- Don't ask rhetorical questions — give your listener a chance to reply.
- Adjust the level of your English to your counterpart's.
- Finally, whatever you may think, booze does *not* make communication smoother or easier.

A Quickie Quiz
Have we raised your level of lingo consciousness?

Within the text you have just finished on lingo were these examples of Americanese that will cause confusion, not clarity, among non-Americans. Did you catch them?

Dr. Seuss
Bazooka gum
Madison Avenue
cornflakes
hoola hoop
Willy Loman
Herschel Walker
EEG
the red eye (flight)
Rodeo Drive
blew out to Catalina
Houstonized
Mary Poppins
King Kong
X-rated
42nd Street
Victor Borge (and his famous phonetic punctuation)
backseat driver

If you spotted these, if you became aware that American colloquialisms were being used in a chapter devoted to becoming more sensitized to them, then score yourself an *A*.

Homework

1. Learn another language.
2. Learn to speak your own language better by *writing* it better.
3. Learn more about the new world to which you are going.

A list of sources for help in all aspects — language, writing, and cross-cultural instruction — can be found in the Appendix.

TURNING THE TIDE

Tips for *Incoming* Visitors to the U.S.

International business traffic flows both ways. So what happens when people from other shores arrive on ours? It can be just as confusing — to both sides — as any cultural breakdown experienced by American innocents abroad. To be sure, many foreigners high up enough in corporate hierarchy to be sent here have almost certainly met their fair share of Americans as well as their own fellow-nationals who have lived and worked here.

Yet a nation's entire ethos and idiosyncrasies cannot be absorbed long-distance. Hence, following are some troublespots for foreigners to anticipate en route.

U.S. Protocol — Business and Personal

What is basically polite and considerate on the other side of the world translates the same way here, with minor variations and perhaps somewhat less emphasis on the formal and decorous.

Timing

U.S. business usually begins on the dot. A nine A.M. appointment means precisely that, except in the most traffic-jammed big cities like New York, Houston, and Los Angeles, where a fifteen-minute delay is rarely frowned upon.

For social engagements, even with business motivations, "drinks at seven" implies something more like seven-thirty. But "dinner at eight" means eight, traffic or no traffic. Business meetings over lunch are the rule rather than the exception and usually start by twelve-thirty and end by two. In America, lunch is rarely a heavy meal of many courses, for the regular workday continues immediately afterwards. Dinner is the main meal, starting between seven and nine unless a cocktail party has preceded it, in which case it might not get going until ten — but rarely later.

Don't be surprised to get breakfast invitations. It is becoming the most popular time of day for intimate business get-togethers and signifies no slight. "Brunch," which is popular on weekends, is a combination meal that starts as early as eleven and can still be had at four. The fare ranges from scrambled eggs to sirloin steak, and the drinks tend to be the fruity-vegi type such as screwdrivers (vodka and orange juice), mimosas (champagne and orange juice), and Bloody Marys (vodka mixed with highly spiced tomato juice). Note: If you wish to be sociable but not imbibe alcohol, one common substitute is a Virgin Mary, or the spiced tomato juice without any alcohol.

No matter what time of day, though, as soon as everyone is seated expect only the briefest exchange of small talk before the Americans get right down to business. No sipping tea or feeling each other out in the U.S.

Hands across the sea

American men invariably shake hands during introductions — women, not as often. *Abrazos*, bowing, and hand-kissing are trotted out only by those who have spent years in another culture where such gestures are common. A peck on the cheek is only exchanged between women or between men and women — and then only after considerable acquaintance.

More and more women are entering the American business world and are making it to some of the highest levels. Women expect the man to let them take the initiative in shaking hands. If the occasion is business, they will almost certainly offer a hand. If it is social, you never know, but it is very rude not to be ready with a hand when invited.

When the chairman isn't

Most businesswomen realize that they are still a novelty to the foreign men they deal with. However, they do not welcome being treated like creatures from another galaxy — or like decoration. The best policy is to ignore gender altogether and proceed as you would with any male colleague. Helping with doors and chairs is fine as long as it does not become too attention-getting. If the woman reaches for the check, react exactly as you would with anyone else: if you are the client, chances are you expect to be treated — so let her do the treating.

With or without others present, never get as personal as you might with a male colleague. And that includes asking about her marital status — leave it to her to establish it, and if she does, a few casual questions about children or husband's occupation are as far as you should go with it.

Needless to say, amorous or suggestive remarks will get you a very cold shoulder 99.9 percent of the time; and can the other .1 percent be worth it?

"Who you?"

In some languages, including English English, "What do you do?" translates as insulting at best. But in America, it is the standard opening line when people meet socially. It means, of course, "What kind of work do you do, and for whom do you do it?" Be prepared for it — it won't go away.

Most businesspeople carry business cards, but in the U.S. they are exchanged not automatically on meeting but usually only if there is some reason to want to get in touch later. No one will refuse *your* card, but do not be offended if you are not given one in return.

When being entertained at an American home, the most common gesture of gratitude is to send a short, informal note to the hostess after the event. Bringing a gift with you is risky, only because it might embarrass other guests who did not. But if you do bring something, potted or cut flowers or a bottle of wine are the safest, although a bouquet of flowers gives the hostess, who will very likely have no hired help, yet another chore just as she is coping with drinks, dinner, and introductions.

Probably the most charming commodity you can come equipped with is a toast or saying from your own culture, to be delivered bilingually as a salute to your host and hostess. It is something they cannot buy at the local supermarket, and invariably they and the other guests lap it up like pink champagne.

To puff or not to puff

In the U.S., land of the five-cent cigar, smoking is becoming as controversial as publicly admitting that you love the president or hate him.

To be on the safe side, either ask if anybody minds or wait to see what the others do. Even some cabdrivers now post signs in the backseat demanding that passengers refrain. A friendly host will seldom do the same, but more and more restaurants are segregating smokers from nonsmokers, which can lead to an awkward decision. If you do and your American host does *not*, do you volunteer to go without a puff all through dinner — or does he sit in a miasma of smoke to accommodate your habit?

No third party can supply the answer (they haven't invented "smoking counselors" yet). You simply have to be sensitive to the other side's position and let your conscience (plus an eye to making a sale) be your guide.

Gestures Here and There

Generally, what signifies "Here's mud in your eye!" where *you* come from has the same impact where *we* come from. Two exceptions you will no doubt encounter are America's "okay" signs. One is thumbs up, and the other is thumb and forefinger joined to form a circle. Either way, don't start punching — the intent is positive. The same is true for the V-for-victory sign, which, fingers facing in or out, never means what it does in Britain.

Patting someone on the rear end is strictly taboo — even though you may see hulking football players do it regularly on TV every Sunday afternoon. (Even then, they mustn't linger.)

But all the other international rudenesses from third finger to forearm jerk have made the trip to the new world intact.

To motion a waiter for the check, make a writing gesture.

To signal to someone he has a telephone call, hold an imaginary phone to your ear.

To wish someone good luck, cross the middle finger over the forefinger.

To wave goodbye, instead of waggling the fingers, move the whole hand from side to side.

One uniquely American gesture as indigenous to some parts of the country as the black fly is the backslap. If it is any consolation to the rest of the world, many Americans dislike it just as much as you do. The best response is a slight but unmistakable wince.

Giving and Entertaining

Giving can be a worse mistake than not giving at all. Americans are still slightly jumpy from the payola scandals of the '70s, and any hint that a business decision might have been influenced by gifts casts a shadow over everyone involved. (After all, the head of the nation's National Security Council lost his job for accepting two Japanese watches.) Even the law discourages excess generosity, placing a $25 limit on the tax deductibility of business gifts.

There are two occasions (other than being entertained in someone's home, which calls for either a thank-you note or a small offering to the hostess such as flowers or wine) when a modest gift is a welcome sign of your cordiality.

One is Christmas Day, December 25, a holiday of traditional gift giving among family, friends, and business associates. If the gift is strictly business, it is best to limit it to something for the office: leather-bound desk diaries, calendars, pen and pencil sets, paperweights, etc. Unless you know the recipient is a teetotaler, liquor or wine is also appropriate. It is customary for the store to Christmas-wrap purchases any time after December 1, so you needn't worry about the right colors (red and green) or designs.

The other reason to give a gift is simply to mark your arrival or departure with a token. Usually, the most appreciated are those from home. *Your* home. Appropriate are something made of jade or other semiprecious native stone; a doily made of handwoven fabric; a national beverage such as aquavit from Scandinavia, pisco sour from Peru, or Armagnac from France; any inexpensive handicraft or artwork; or an illustrated book about your country, its people, or its art. Cheap trinkets from *any*where are an insult, especially when imprinted with your company's logo. This is like foisting a piece of advertising promotion on your host.

If the businessperson you are dealing with over here is a woman, avoid personal gifts such as perfume, clothing (except perhaps a scarf or handkerchief), and makeup. If you know before leaving home that you will meet your host's family, it is always appropriate to take a small homegrown gift for spouse or children: a silver coin from Mexico, *niello* from Thailand, carved animal figures, or a cookbook of native dishes if you know the recipient can read your language.

Business gifts should be given after negotiations are over, preferably on a social occasion like a last lunch or farewell drink. If the present is a personal one, never offer it while others are on hand unless it is well known that you and the recipient are old and close friends.

Don't be insulted if an American does not reciprocate immediately. It may not happen until you have returned home — or come back on your next trip. There is no particular time limit here for returning favors.

Probably the most common gift given and received in the U.S. is entertainment, a word that covers everything from a quick drink to a weekend at a resort. It in no way signifies that you must return tit for tat. Not only is it tax-deductible but it will no doubt go on your host's expense account. The proper response is a sincere thank-you and an offer to return the favor when your host visits you.

POSTSCRIPT

There is one universal action, one signal, one form of communication that is used and understood by every culture and in every country, no matter how remote.

It can help you with every relationship — business or personal — and become the single most useful form of communication.

It is . . . the smile.

We hope that this book has brought you one or two of those.

Among all the do's and don'ts in international travel, the smile is a gigantic "do." It will help you through the toughest of times and make your travel or transactions the stimulating fun and challenge they should be.

THE EDITOR

APPENDIX

Sources
of
Help

Learning Another Language

Learning a second language presupposes that most of your business travels will be in one area where one language predominates. And not even a total-immersion course will produce results overnight. In fact, there is no teacher nearly as effective as living with the language in its own land.

Of course, there are less drastic alternatives. In the Manhattan telephone book alone, 79 different language schools are listed, not including individual tutors. Berlitz has branches in over 200 locations in the U.S. and elsewhere and is now developing a whole new curriculum of programs in cross-cultural training and orientation. For those in a hurry, there is a nine-hour-a-day, five-day-a-week program that lasts from two to six weeks. You emerge frazzled but reasonably fluent.

Most community colleges and universities and even some high schools with adult-education classes offer courses — usually in Western European languages. But people with demanding full-time jobs often find private tutoring the most flexible way to learn.

Schools and organizations that offer language instruction as well as a variety of cross-cultural training programs for business executives traveling abroad include: the *American Graduate School of International Management* in Glendale, Arizona (see page 173); the *School for International Training* in Brattleboro, Vermont (see page 175); American University's *Business Council for International Understanding Institute* in Washington, D.C. (see page 173); and *Transemantics, Inc.* in Washington, D.C. (see page 176).

Don't assume that because your company has never volunteered to underwrite employees' language lessons they would not be open to at least sharing the cost. For starters, you might ask them to buy a do-it-yourself cassette kit, which you and others in the firm could use as a warm-up — and to prove that you are serious about learning.

Speak Your Language Better
By Writing It Better

The better we write, the better we talk. Writing good business English comes not from acquiring technical skills but from organizing our thinking.

Again, local schools from preparatory to college level offer courses, and only one or two semesters in an extension program should be enough for most businesspeople to be writing — and speaking — a new brand of English. It is, however, a subject that many college graduates have no trouble teaching themselves. All you need is patience and a good book. Here is a list of some of the best books on the subject recently published or reissued.

Books on Writing

The Art of Writing Clearly; W. G. Ryckman; Dow Jones-Irwin Personal Learning Aid Series; 1983. This book takes you from the fundamentals of word usage to the fine art of writing lucid business reports.

The Elements of Style; William Strunk, Jr., and E. B. White; Macmillan; 1979. This is the book that "wrote the book" on the elements of style. It would be hard to find any book on any subject that says so much so well in just 92 paperback-size pages.

English English: A Descriptive Dictionary; Norman W. Schur; Verbatim; 1980. A must for anyone headed for the U.K., the book catalogs the colorful pitfalls of finding yourself in the land of the Queen's English, from *damp squib* to a *surgical spirit.*

The Well-Tempered Sentence; Karen Elizabeth Gordon; Ticknor & Fields; 1983 and *The Transitive Vampire;* Karen Elizabeth Gordon; Times Books; 1984. Both of these slim but nourishing little volumes are subtitled *A Handbook of Grammar for the Innocent, the Eager & the Doomed.* Whether you fall into any or all of those categories, these whimsically illustrated books prove that grammar and punctuation can be more bizarre than boring.

Writing Out Loud: A Self-Help Guide to Clear Business Writing; Dr. John L. DiGaetani, Jane Boisseau DiGaetani, and Prof. Earl N. Harbert; Dow Jones-Irwin; 1983. This is a clear, concise handbook on improving writing skills by using your natural conversational instincts.

Writing that Works; Kenneth Roman and Joel Raphaelson; Harper & Row; 1981. Two top advertising writers with Ogilvy & Mather have written a book just the way the title says it should be.

Learn About
The New World You Are Visiting

Columbus may have been the best known traveler who didn't know where he was going, but he wasn't the last. We think nothing of flying for twenty hours at supersonic speeds only to reach a land that is a total political, cultural, and geographical blank to us.

While increasing numbers of American firms are starting to take the mystery out of the Mysterious East (and West) with employee indoctrination courses, all too often they are reserved for those going to live there. There is also, however, hope for those who are just visiting.

Training: Workshops, Instruction, Lectures, and Other Information Sources

The American Graduate School of International Management (Glendale, Arizona), also known as the Thunderbird School, was founded in 1946 by a group of international-minded citizens led by a lieutenant general determined to solve the problem of innocents abroad who were not prepared for international assignments. In addition to stressing foreign-language training, the school gives customized, concentrated programs embracing the whole spectrum of foreign culture shock. Cultural programs can be arranged for a few days up to weeks or months. Intensive language courses take six to eight weeks.

James Bostain (Alexandria, Virginia), a linguist and former trainer for the U.S. Department of State language school, has won Emmy awards for his television programs on what he calls "cross-cultural consciousness-raising." He delivers these same lectures live to groups from coast to coast.

The Business Council for International Understanding at American University (Washington, D.C.) trains both Americans and foreign nationals to operate in other cultures. With over 25,000 graduates from technicians to corporate C.E.O.s in 125 countries, it is the oldest organization in the business. Programs are custom-designed and run by American University faculty, all with experience and expertise in specific areas. They can be arranged for individuals, executives and their families, and for larger groups. The basic course is intercultural communication training, but there are also area studies, language training, and special sessions in business practices of specific areas.

Cultural Orientation Services, Inc., (609 Second Avenue, Minneapolis, Minnesota) fields a network of specialists who conduct programs for traveling executives and their families covering creative listening, communicative speaking, and cultural differences. A complete program lasts no longer than two or three days. "Introduction to Life in the United States" is a program that helps foreign families adapt to U.S. culture.

The Department of Development of the State of Ohio, International Trade Services Division (Columbus, Ohio), offers excellent research and information services both at home and in Brussels and Tokyo. Its trade specialists work with Ohio companies to help them expand and improve exports and obtain the latest data on banking and financing exports. Other benefits include establishing overseas contacts and cutting red tape.

Going International, a consulting service (San Francisco, California), has produced a series of films and videotapes to help the American traveler become more effective in international business. Parts I and II focus on cultural differences in business. Part III deals with cultural shock and the expatriate's family. Part IV deals with unexpected difficulties that employees and families experience upon returning to the U.S.

The Institute for Intercultural Communication at Stanford University (Palo Alto, California) concentrates primarily on Japan but also prepares managers for other Asian assignments. To illustrate the program's breadth, here is the current curriculum: orientations to Japanese culture; essentials of Japanese language; adapting to life in Tokyo; English for intercultural communication; communicating through interpretation; family adaptation in Japan; Japanese business culture; comparative management styles; negotiating with Japanese; intercultural effectiveness in business. Stanford's Institute also offers annual training workshops for professionals doing business in multinational environments.

The Intercultural Press (Yarmouth, Maine) not only publishes extensively on the subject (see page 176) but also provides consultation in setting up multicultural organizations and departments of organizations or joint ventures with company nationals from two or more nations. Issues such as supervisory styles and patterns of communication are explored and resolved by the counseling arm of this organization.

The International Business Center of New England (Boston, Massachusetts) sponsors meetings and workshops on the specifics of exporting as well as such subjects as "The Role of Translation Service Organizations" and "Effective Cross-Cultural Orientation."

The Massachusetts Port Authority (Massport) (Boston, Massachusetts) has spawned the Small Business Export Program for businesses throughout the six New England states. Staffs in Boston, London, and Tokyo offer individualized instruction in selling overseas. They also arrange trade missions so manufacturers can establish contracts, schedule appointments, make travel reservations, obtain translators, and convert currencies — all in advance. Massport even provides interest-free loans to help cover travel expenses. In early 1985, Massport will unveil its computerized "International Marketing Information Service" in order to better serve the information needs of the growing New England export community.

Middle East Specialists (Austin, Texas) provides orientation in history, religion, family, language, legalities, Arab business practices and private life, as well as in general cultural differences and difficulties. Programs are shaped to meet the participant's specific needs and typically last three days.

Renwick and Associates Incorporated (Carefree, Arizona) prepares clients for international business in training sessions that last from two days to two weeks.

The School for International Training (Brattleboro, Vermont) is the academic offshoot of the celebrated Experiment in International Living, founded in 1932. The school offers undergraduate and graduate degree programs in addition to short-term training for corporate executives; courses are tailor-made to each participant's goals.

SIETAR International publishes intercultural training books, a newsletter, and a journal. The latter two are included in membership, along with discounts on publications and programs. (See also page 175.)

Trans-Cultural Services (180 Ravenhill Drive, Orinda, California) specializes in relocation and cross-cultural communications for Europe, the Middle East, Indonesia, and the Pacific Basin. Training is area-specific and conducted by both natives of the country and Americans who have lived and/or worked there recently. In addition, participants gain practical information for everyday concerns and valuable business contacts abroad.

Transemantics, Inc. (1828 L Street, Washington, D.C.) maintains briefing and language centers in three capital locations and also sends trainers anywhere in the U.S. Programs are tailored to particular needs and presented by an area expert and a cultural representative who can act out potential real-life problems with participants. (See also *International Language Institute*, page 177.)

Communication Services, Helpful Publications

The Center for International and Area Studies of Brigham Young University (Provo, Utah) supplies quick studies in the challenges of international travel. Booklets include *Jet Lag and Decision Making*, *Questions Asked about America*, and *Intercultural Communicating*. Also useful are the four-page briefings called *Culturgrams*, which detail the customs, manners, likes, and dislikes of the peoples of 81 countries.

The District Export Council in your area of the U.S. is a group of experienced international business executives, appointed by the U.S. Secretary of Commerce, who volunteer their services. Contact the nearest district office of the Department of Commerce.

Intercom, a department of the *American Graduate School of International Management*, conducts research studies and surveys on subjects such as technology transfer and legal and political restrictions overseas. (See also *The American Graduate School of International Management*, page 173.)

The Intercultural Press publishes a long list of valuable guides, including *Survival Kit for Overseas Living; International Negotiation: A Cross-Cultural Perspective*; and *The Management of Intercultural Relations in International Business: A Directory of Resources*. They also put out two popular series. One is titled *Update* and covers the globe from Bahrain to West Germany (how to prepare to leave home, what to do on arrival, local regulations and business practices, etc.). The other series is called *Interacts* and analyzes how we do things differently from other peoples and how relationships are thus affected. (See also page 174-175.)

The International Language Institute of Transemantics, Inc. stresses the study of *kinesics,* or body language, as a key to effective understanding of others. But the institute also offers multilanguage support from translating and interpreting to multilingual typesetting, promotional and technical writing and editing, film and tape narration, and convention services. Staff experts also conduct research services from cartography to feasibility studies and environmental impact records. Information is held in strictest confidence whenever requested. (See also *Transemantics, Inc.,* page 176.)

OmniLingua, Inc. (2857 Mount Vernon Road, S.E., Cedar Rapids, Iowa, and 6 North Michigan Avenue, Chicago, Illinois) translates, typesets, and prints manuals, audiovisuals, and materials-ads. All work is checked for technical accuracy, grammar, and local flavor.

SIETAR International publishes intercultural training books, a newsletter, and a journal. The latter two are included in membership, along with discounts on publications and programs. (See also page 175.)

The Stanford Institute for Intercultural Communication (see page 174) publishes an extensive directory of selected resources on other cultures, including training services and publishers.

One final source of names and addresses you can turn to overseas is the *consulate or trade mission* here of the nation you are visiting there. The trail can be circuitous — but worth it. For example, if you call the commercial office of the New York Consulate of the People's Republic of China, you will be given the name and address of the China United Trading Corporation, Ltd., in New York, which in turn will give you the name and address of the people you really want to talk to — China Trade Consultation and Technical Service Corp., Andingmenway, Beijing, China.

The Business Traveller's Handbook; Foseco Minsep Group, compiler; Prentice-Hall; 1983. Foseco Minsep, which is involved in a number of business activities, compiled information for this handbook from its international travelers. The book, which is subtitled *How to Get Along with People in 100 Countries,* provides tips on protocol and etiquette, including correct forms of address, clothing, entertainment, tipping, table manners, and more.

Enterprise and Development, a four-page monthly newsletter published by the U.S. Council for International Business (1212 Avenue of the Americas, New York, New York) gives news of international enterprises and provides brief summaries of books, speeches, and research projects on the international business scene.

Going International; Random House; 1985. A guide for the international businessperson on how to make friends, win deals, manage people, and generally get things done in the foreign country.

Helping Across Cultures; Gordon L. Lippitt and David S. Hoopes, editors; International Consultants Foundation; contains an eye-opening Culture Shock Test that reveals how ready you really are to deal with the rest of the world. The grade you get will tell you how much of the help described here you need.

Key Officers of Foreign Service Posts - Guide for Business Representatives — of all the books, courses, and self-help you ply yourself with, none will probably prove more valuable than this modest little handbook. The title is a mouthful — the contents are a godsend. Compiled by the State Department, available for sale by the Superintendent of Documents, U.S. Government Printing Office, Washington, D.C. 20402 (ask for Publication #7877), and released in January 1983, the guide contains names, addresses, and telephone numbers of all commercial officers, chiefs of missions, financial attachés, political officers, labor officers, consular officers, regional security officers, scientific attachés, agricultural officers, and cultural affairs specialists in countries worldwide. It also lists U.S. Department of Commerce district offices throughout this country. (A call or visit to your nearest district office should precede any business trip you make abroad as a first — and vital — point of contact for foreign trade.)

Multinational Executive Travel Companion — Business Travel Tips Worldwide is revised and published annually by Multinational Executive, Inc., a service of Guides to Multinational Business, Inc., Boston, Massachusetts. This handy paperback guidebook lists trade fairs and exhibitions, currencies and electric current, and facts and tips on customs in various countries.

The Traveler's Guide to European Customs & Manners; Nancy L. Braganti and Elizabeth DeVine; Meadowbrook; 1984. Subtitle of this book is *How to converse, dine, tip, drive, bargain, dress, make friends and conduct business while in Europe.*

INDEX